STRENGTHEN
SOCIETY IN

POSSIBILITIES AND DILEMMAS FOR
INTERNATIONAL NGOS

Edited by

BURMA CENTER NETHERLANDS (BCN)
TRANSNATIONAL INSTITUTE (TNI)

SILKWORM BOOKS

First published in 1999 by
Silkworm Books
54/1 Sridonchai Road, Chiang Mai 50100, Thailand.
E-mail: silkworm@pobox.com

Cover photograph by BCN
Set in 11 pt. Garamond

Printed by O.S. Printing House, Bangkok.

CONTENTS

INTRODUCTION

Burma's political deadlock has still to be resolved. At the time of this writing, Aung San Suu Kyi is sitting in her car at a roadblock just outside of Rangoon. The roadblock was put up by the army to prevent her from meeting fellow party members of the National League for Democracy (NLD). According to the state-run newspapers, the NLD is Burma's "enemy number one." The junta's uncompromising stand in the whole affair, and its refusal to start a dialogue, is drawing criticism from the rest of the world, including, significantly, from some ASEAN members. Philippine foreign minister Domingo Siazon called on all parties in Burma to start negotiations without preconditions and to initiate the process of national reconciliation. Such open criticism would have been unthinkable even a year ago.

In July 1998, at the annual meeting of foreign ministers of ASEAN, Thailand, supported by the Philippines, pushed for the inclusion of controversial issues such as democracy and human rights in the agenda. Thai foreign minister Surin Pitsuwan suggested introducing a policy of "flexible engagement" because these are the issues "we have to increasingly deal with in our engagement with the outside world." Indonesia, Malaysia, and Singapore on the other hand spoke out strongly against the Thai proposal, saying this would contradict ASEAN's fundamental principle of non-interference in the internal affairs of member states.

These policy contradictions, however, indicate that the continuing repression of people's rights to organize outside the state structure in countries like Burma, and to a lesser extent in Indonesia, Malaysia, and Singapore, is a serious threat to the freedoms achieved in other parts of Southeast Asia. Burma's admission into ASEAN last year is a leading example. The expansion of ASEAN to include more non-democratic regimes could help neutralize the influence of formal democratic regimes with strong civil societies, such as the Philippines and Thailand, within ASEAN and in the region.

Burma's membership is also causing serious problems for ASEAN's relations with the EU. The EU has so far refused to let Burma officially take part in its meetings with ASEAN because of its appalling human rights record and its refusal to begin a process of democratization. As a result of this, a number of EU-ASEAN meetings have been canceled and postponed. With the current financial crisis in the region far from being resolved, Burma's internal problems have now also started to worry ASEAN.

Burma's foreign relations with Europe are currently predominantly confined to the economic field. After years of self-imposed isolation which ruined the country's economy, and forced it to apply for LDC (Least Developed Country) status, Burma opened its doors again for foreign investment in 1988. To what extent the country will open up socially and politically and to what extent people-to-people relations between Europe and Burma can be established still remains to be seen.

Among European non-governmental organizations (NGOs), there is a growing interest in working in Burma or on issues related to Burma. This increased interest generates a need to study carefully the conditions under which international NGO initiatives are allowed to take place in Burma, a country in which both the social and economic sectors are dominated by the military.

What is the present state of civil society in Burma, and how can one develop strategies to strengthen civil society as an essential element in the growth of pluralism and democratization? These were some of the key questions posed at the conference "Civil Society in Burma: Possibilities and Dilemmas for International NGOs," organized by the Transnational Institute (TNI) and the Burma Center Netherlands (BCN), with the financial support of Novib and Hivos, in December 1997.

This book presents the main papers discussed at this conference. The authors examine different aspects of civil society in central Burma and the ethnic minority areas, the legal aspects of freedom of association in Burma, and the questions surrounding the debate on the role of international non-governmental organizations (INGOs). It is by no means a complete study of civil society in Burma or the manner in which the international community can establish links and stimulate the process towards peace and democratization. Rather, it is an attempt to identify the embryonic state of civil society in Burma, and to describe the recent developments that are taking place on the ground.

David Steinberg provides an analysis of the concept of civil society and its place in Burmese history in the first chapter. Steinberg believes that civil society, broadly defined as those institutions and groupings outside of the state, is one of the critical elements in the growth of both pluralism and democracy. In traditional Burmese society, he identifies religious organizations at the local level as the most obvious examples of civil society institutions.

Following independence, civil society did develop in Burma, although it occurred mainly in the urban areas and had close links with the government. He notes that even during the "caretaker government" (1958–1960) civil society continued to exist. This changed dramatically when the military gained power in 1962, and created a one-party state ruled by the Burma Socialist Program Party (BSPP), who took control of almost all private organizations. The BSPP not only dominated all social activity, but also made great efforts to influence and coerce support from the public. "Civil society," writes Steinberg, "died under the Burma Socialist Program Party (BSPP); perhaps, more accurately, it was murdered."

The coup of September 1988 which brought the State Law and Order Restoration Council (SLORC) to power was, according to Steinberg, merely a cosmetic move since there was no actual transfer of power. Steinberg finds that the concept of the nature of power and its structural organization remained unchanged throughout the BSPP and SLORC periods, but argues that there have been changes in the way the state has responded to both mass mobilization and civil society. The BSPP era was characterized by the requirement that all military and civilian personnel of the government join the party, which became the only means to career advancement. The SLORC has gone further and created its own civil society organization, the Union Solidarity and Development Association (USDA). Steinberg argues that pluralism will eventually expand in Burma, but concludes that the immediate future for civil society in Burma remains bleak.

In the second chapter Martin Smith examines civil society in the context of the long-running ethnic conflict in Burma. This conflict, he argues, is one of the most critical problems facing Burma today and one which cannot be separated from reform in the social, political, and economic spheres.

Smith argues that although the current deadlock has yet to be resolved and the military is still firmly in control, it is important to realize that the political landscape in Burma has changed in the past decade. The 1990 elections and the cease-fire movement stand out as the most important examples of this change according to Smith. Smith argues that there is no one prescriptive model for signposting the road to peace, reform and development. Instead, international agencies should analyze the situation on the ground, taking into account both the causes and dynamics of the suffering and conflict at the local level, and examine the institutional and social problems from a "ground-up" perspective. By doing this, two dominant problems facing Burma emerge: ethnic conflict and the weakness of the state. Since independence in 1948 the Burmese state has fueled rather than healed the strong social and ethnic divisions in Burma.

Smith believes that there is potential for greater international access to Burma's ethnic minority regions, which he refers to as "war-affected areas." He separates developments which have taken place as a result of the ceasefires in these "war-affected areas" into the political and social dimensions. If civil society is to develop, he writes, there needs to be official political recognition of the nationalist movements which represent the will of their people. It is of great importance that every sector of society is empowered and involved. Therefore INGOs need to engage with all actors within Burmese society, including political parties, indigenous NGOs, religious and ethnic organizations, as well as state institutions.

Zunetta Liddell gives an overview of the legal aspects of freedom of association in Burma, the repercussions people face in failing to obey these laws, and what actually happens despite the legal restrictions. Burma, she writes, is a highly authoritarian state where people are not able to enjoy the fundamental freedoms upon which the development and maintenance of civil society depends, such as freedom of thought, opinion, association, and movement.

After noting that there is a lack of clarity and openness in Burma's legal system, an absence of an independent and impartial judiciary and the operation of due process of law, Liddell proceeds to describe a number of notorious laws limiting basic freedoms.

According to Liddell, any moves towards developing a civil society can take place only at the most local level. She identifies such possibilities in those "ephemeral events" which are not perceived as a threat by the state. These events include village level activities by church congregations or Buddhist monasteries, or town and state level activities such as temple festivals, emergency relief work, national immunization campaigns, and so on.

Liddell concludes that the prospects for the development of civil society in Burma are not promising. Even without the military government and its pervasive military intelligence agents, it would take a major shift in ways of thinking and working, beginning at the level of education, for civil society to really take root and prosper. Fundamental to this process would be a relaxing of media censorship.

In the final chapter, Marc Purcell examines the question surrounding the debate on INGO involvement in Burma. He addresses the issues facing INGOs who want to work on Burma, the possibilities that could be explored for facilitating civil society, and the attitude INGOs should adopt towards the democracy movement inside Burma.

A substantial part of this chapter deals with the debate over whether or not INGOs should work in Burma at all, the type of programs undertaken by these agencies in Burma and the problems they face. Purcell argues that INGOs should consult with Aung San Suu Kyi and the NLD about their programs in Burma. He also finds that since a majority of the ethnic armed opposition groups have brokered ceasefires with SLORC and some are calling for aid and development assistance from the international community, it is increasingly difficult to maintain the position that INGOs should not be in Burma.

If civil society is to be nurtured in Burma, he writes, it is crucial for INGOs to initiate development strategies which foster independent and democratic thinking among the communities they target and the staff they employ. In working with these communities INGOs need to adopt a broad body of principles on what community development should mean in the Burmese context. While the term "empowerment" cannot be used openly, he concludes that this must be the final outcome of the process of development.

In conclusion, the articles in this collection show that despite some changes in Burma's political landscape since 1988, the initiatives of civil society remain severely repressed.

Recent demonstrations, however, by students and NLD youth continue to challenge the Burmese military regime. Their demands for democratic change is a strong testament to the Burmese people's desire for a political system which is not built on the use of force and intimidation, but makes a space for civil society to develop.

Burma Center Netherlands   Tom Kramer
Transnational Institute   Pietje Vervest

ABOUT THE AUTHORS

DAVID I. STEINBERG is director of Asian studies at Georgetown University, and a consultant to the Asia Foundation. He is the author of three volumes on Burma, and over thirty articles on aspects of that society. He lived in Burma for four years and studied Burmese and Southeast Asia at the School of Oriental and African Studies, University of London. He was educated at Dartmouth College, Lingnan University (China), and Harvard University. He has served as director of technical assistance for Asia and the Middle East in the US Agency for International Development, as president of the Mansfield Center for Pacific Affairs, and as representative of the Asia Foundation for Korea. He has lived in Asia for over seventeen years.

MARTIN SMITH is a writer and journalist specializing on Burmese and ethnic nationality affairs. He is author of *Burma: Insurgency and the Politics of Ethnicity* (Zed Books, London, 1991 [2nd edition: 1998]), *Ethnic Groups in Burma: Development, Democracy and Human Rights* (Anti-Slavery International, London, 1994), and *Fatal Silence? Freedom of Expression and the Right to Health in Burma* (Article 19, London, 1996). His television work includes the documentaries, *Burma: Dying for Democracy* (Channel Four UK, 1989), and *Forty Million Hostages* (BBC, 1991).

ZUNETTA LIDDELL was until August 1998 the Burma researcher for Human Rights Watch/Asia. She has also worked as a consultant to Amnesty International and the U.N. Center for Human Rights. She spent eighteen months in Burma during 1988–1989 where she was conducting research for a post-graduate degree. She has traveled frequently to Burma, Thailand, and Bangladesh since then, and continues to work as a freelance consultant on Burma.

MARC PURCELL is an activist and development worker currently serving as African Regional Program Officer for the Overseas Service Bureau. From 1995 to 1997 he headed the Australian Council for Overseas Aid's Burma project which conducted human rights advocacy on Burma. In addition to regular visits to the Thai Burma border, he has spent time in Rangoon working in the areas of social work and community health. He has a master's degree in Burmese history from Monash University.

A VOID IN MYANMAR: CIVIL SOCIETY IN BURMA[1]

DAVID I. STEINBERG

The term "civil society" has been prominent in the history of Western intellectual thought for about two hundred years. Its connotative vicissitudes, its origins and previous political uses from Hegel and Marx and beyond, in a sense, reflect a microcosm both of political and social science theory. For a period, reflection on civil society was out of style, an anachronistic concept replaced by more fashionable intellectual formulations. Today, however, the term has once again come back into significance. Here, however, we are not concerned with its history, but rather with its contemporary use as defined below, as one means to understand the dynamics of Burmese politics and society.

CIVIL SOCIETY AND THE STATE

Although civil society developed in Europe, scholars worldwide have been restudying the question of civil society and its past influence on and potential relevance to the contemporary political and social scenes in their cultures. They sometimes look for indigenous roots of civil society within their own cultures and histories even though the concept was unknown, and are sometimes successful, although the modern variants may be quite different from historical precedents.

A multitude of contemporary definitions of "civil society" abound; writers adapt the term to their particular predilections. What is important is not the search for one absolute definition applicable across all states—the "one size fits all" syndrome—but that we have a clear and distinct concept of what we mean and the analytical ends to which we employ the concept.

Civil society obviously means those institutions and groupings that are outside of government. There are nuances in different definitions, but the essential characteristic of what we call civil society lies in its autonomy from government. It is also obvious that such independence is relative, and as no individual can be isolated, so no institution within a societal framework stands completely alone. The significance of the term today and its importance as an analytical tool to explore societies lie in the hypothesis that if civil society is strong and if citizens band together for the common good based on a sense of community or programmatic trust and efficacy, then this trust and efficacy somehow translate into overall trust in the political process of democracy or democratization and lead to diffusion of the centralized power of the state. Civil society is thus an essential element of political pluralism—the diffusion of power that is the hallmark of modern democracies.

In fact, many argue that civil society is a critical element of democracy. So democracy is not simply free and fair elections, which are a manifestation of part of the process yet in the popular eye are often equated with democracy, but rather democracy is composed of a variety of diverse institutions including a system of a universal adult electorate, an elected legislature, an independent judiciary, a free press and media, and civil society—the ability of citizens to gather together in groups to express their common concerns. Parenthetically, then, the May 1990 elections in Burma were important when considering the issue of democracy in that country, but certainly not a reflection of more complex phenomena.

These independent groups under an all-encompassing definition might include opposition political parties, the business sector or for-profit organizations, the non-profit groups, and even those elements bent on the overthrow of the government through non-elective processes. It is, thus, no wonder that in many societies, such as China, the term civil society implies anti-government activity, and thus its use is deemed inappropriate. This, I would argue, misconstrues the importance and place of civil society in much of the world, and is not helpful to our analysis of Burmese issues.

For purposes of definition in the case of Burma/Myanmar, civil society is best more narrowly defined. Here it is used as composed of those non-ephemeral organizations of individuals banded together for a common purpose or purposes to pursue those interests through group activities and by peaceful means. These are generally non-profit organizations, and may be local or national, advocacy or supportive, religious, cultural, social, professional, educational, or even organizations that, while not for profit, support the business sector, such as chambers of commerce, trade associations, etc.

We are excluding from this definition in the case of Burma/ Myanmar businesses, political parties, and groups that are engaged in insurgent activities. However important these may be, they deserve consideration under other rubrics. They are included in more broad definitions, and were especially important in the rise of pluralistic centers of power divorced from the thrones of Europe. The bourgeoisie played a particularly critical role there. Political parties and the business community in contemporary Myanmar are excluded because those political parties that are legal are severely circumscribed by the state and cannot operate independent of government power and considerable control or restrictions, the indigenous business sector is still nascent and developing within the government's formal and informal strictures, and all insurgent groups are excluded because civil society under this definition operates within the legal bounds of state laws and regulations and does not attempt to overthrow state authority.

The importance of civil society is that included groups have the capacity to act or advocate, autonomous of the state, for the common good, however defined and over how large a clientele—national, local, or specialized. They provide sources of pluralism in the society, thus diluting the possibility of a completely centralized, autocratic, or authoritarian state. They are not the only potential source of pluralism—this may come from the division of powers among elements of government, even within the executive branch itself and sometimes between that branch and the government's political party in power. But they are an important source.

These organizations may span the spectrum of state relationships: they may advocate policies that support the government (if they are not its captive), they may call for stricter adherence to laws already enacted, call for new laws or activities, express interest in restructuring elements of policy, or simply do what its members regard as good, such as upholding traditional values or protecting the environment. For example, in Myanmar a village organization that was formed independently of the state to make offerings to the monks at a local temple would be part of civil society, but the hierarchy of the *sangha*, which is registered and is under state control, would not be so considered. An organization may have to be registered by the government (in Burma, under the Companies Act, for example), but it could be part of civil society if it were autonomous in its actions, and if its leadership were not subservient to, or chosen by, the state. It is conceivable that a private organization in part funded by the state might be within the bounds of civil society under this definition if it operated autonomously of the government. How autonomous must an organization be to qualify? It will depend on the culture and circumstances—how much space does the state allow between its role in intervening into the lives and activities of its citizenry, the extent of the privacy of the individual, and the autonomy of organizations.

In some societies, such as those evolving from the Confucian tradition in which the state is idealistically presented as the benevolent father intervening for the good of his children—the people—that space tends to be quite narrow. In others, the gap is quite wide. In post-Confucian societies, not only does the state presume that intervention is appropriate and even necessary, but the citizenry also believes that some extensive degree of intervention is also desirable. This has important implications for human rights policies that are universally mandated. Concepts of privacy are culturally determined.

Civil society is often viewed as a threat by autocratic governments or those that do not wish to see their policies or programs undermined or even questioned. For this reason, and to preclude the development and influence of such organizations even if they are allowed to be formed, the state will often sponsor mass organizations that are designed both to provide a popular or mass base for state policies, or to preempt the formation of other groups that might oppose or threaten such policies.

CIVIL SOCIETY IN BURMA

I know of no research on civil society, as such, in traditional Burma, although my search of the literature is no doubt incomplete. There would be those who could argue that such organizations existed, or even were prevalent, in the pre-colonial period. The whole structure of the village headman system, for example, might be construed as an element of civil society designed to ward off interference by the state in village affairs. It was transformed by the British from the highest level of local organization to the lowest level of central administration, thus changing its functions and roles.[2]

The quintessential example of civil society ubiquitous throughout Burmese history have been religious organizations at the local level. The act of people willingly and spontaneously gathering together to support local Buddhist activities connected with the seasonal ceremonies came to form an integral part of the social and religious scene. Since the British did not allow overtly political organizations, religion (a primordial loyalty closely associated with nationalism) became a natural focus for organizational activities both for religious good works and patriotic activities. The Young Men's Buddhist Association (modeled after and in competition with the YMCA) was one such group, with both social welfare and advocacy activities, at the national level involved in the independence movement. Organizations of this type continue to the present, and they have been supplemented by other religious-oriented groups formed, especially beginning with the colonial era, to provide ethnic/religious solidarity among Christian, Muslim, and Hindu communities. Many of these organizations conducted social welfare activities often beyond the confines of their own immediate membership.

There has been a lack of scholarship on many of the aspects of modern, independent Burma/Myanmar, first, because of the nature of the insurgencies that limited physical access virtually since independence, then because of government policies that prevented field research by both indigenous and foreign scholars. That problem continues, so our knowledge is fractional at best. Yet the few studies published indicate that at the village level Burmese generally did not join together for civil society functions except for religious purposes, but that such organizations were extensive.

Civil society did develop under republican Burma. It seems to have been basically an urban phenomenon, except for the religious groups that continued in the villages but were also prevalent in the cities, many of which were socially extended, agglutinated villages. Professional and other organizations were formed and flourished in an era where considerable space did exist between the state and the society. That space was somewhat circumscribed because of three factors: the heritage of laws from the colonial period that were used to suppress political dissent and the independence movement, the insurgencies that prompted immediate concerns for state security, and a tradition in which state intervention was countenanced. Social space did, however, exist. There were, of course, close, interpenetrating links between the civil society groups and the government. This was to be expected, because with a relatively small elite group and an extended family system, the relationships between the private and public spheres were often close. In politics as well, there were in the past close familial ties between members of the insurgencies and the government at the highest levels.

In addition to the formation of civil society, however, the government (and the political opposition as well) mobilized the citizenry through the generation of mass organizations linked to the political process.

The Anti-Fascist People's Freedom League (AFPFL) was the umbrella organization under which coalitions and factions existed to rule the state since independence. Formed first against the Japanese at the close of World War II, and then spearheading the independence movement, the AFPFL dominated politics. The violent left wing went underground in revolt, the Karen were in rebellion, and the alternative to the AFPFL was the legitimate, far left-wing party, the National Unity Front (NUF).

Professional and non-political organizations flourished, but since most employment of the educated population was directly or indirectly linked to government, these organizations, although independent, were in the mainstream of Burmese life. The AFPFL spawned a wide range of mass organizations designed to mobilize society for ends determined by the AFPFL, and to keep them in power. The All Burma Peasant's Organization and the All Burma Worker's Organization were just two of many groups with extensive membership that allowed the party to perpetuate itself in power, and to foster the individual roles of its leadership. One of the avenues of social mobility in Burma at that time (along with free education, the military, and the sangha) was through the leadership of such mass organizations. These organizations under state control could not be considered part of civil society, but were rather extensions of state power.

As a coalition, the AFPFL was riddled with factional and separate interests within the leadership. This led in 1958 to the split between groups known as the "Clean" and "Stable" AFPFL that pushed Burma to the verge of civil war, at which point the military virtually forced a constitutional "coup" that ended by giving the army about eighteen months to run and clean up the country.

The first military intervention (1958–1960) was known as the "caretaker government." The military promised to return the state to civilian control, which it did after fair elections in 1960 that returned U Nu to office, a return that the army did not want and failed to predict (shades of military ignorance of popular feeling in 1990). Rule at this time was autocratic, presaging much of what happened after the coup of 1988. Squatters were moved out of Rangoon to newly created suburbs, the military intervened into the economy by founding businesses that still continue as well as by attempting to control prices in the bazaar. The military occupied most critical posts in the state administration, and conducted foreign policy as well, reaching agreement with China on a border settlement. The army stripped the Shan sawbwas of their power, and introduced universal male and female military conscription, which was never enforced because the number of volunteers exceeded need.

At this time the army also engaged in extensive mass mobilization efforts, such as the National Solidarity Associations, to form groups supportive of its policies. Extensive anti-communist propaganda campaigns were conducted by the psychological warfare division of the military. But, as in the AFPFL period, civil society did exist, and the military made no effort to enforce complete mobilization of the populace.

The election of U Nu and the triumph of his party introduced an ineffectual government that seemed as much mystical as it was developmental. U Nu ordered 70,000 sand pagodas to be built to ward off disaster to the country, and the prominence of Buddhism as a state religion, which had been a campaign promise much opposed by the military, made some of the minorities restive. The military perceived that the threats to the unity of the state (due to compromise provisions of the 1947 constitution that unrealistically allowed the Shan and Kayah states to opt out of the Union of Burma after a ten year hiatus and a plebiscite) were so extreme as to prompt the coup of 2 March,

1962 that served to perpetuate military rule in that state. Some claim that the military was in any case bent on power, and this was the convenient excuse to assume control under the guise of the ever-popular slogan of the unity of the state—a slogan that reappeared with vigor under the SLORC.

THE BURMA SOCIALIST PROGRAM PARTY (1962–1988)

Civil society died under the Burma Socialist Program Party (BSPP); perhaps, more accurately, it was murdered. The military ruled by decree until 1974 through a Revolutionary Council of a few officers led by General Ne Win, who had been commander of the armed forces since 1949. The BSPP was formed as a small cadre of military within four months of the coup. All other political activity was prohibited as the military slowly built up the BSPP from a coterie of Ne Win supporters to a mass mobilization system that had its first party congress in 1971. The constitution of 1974 mandated a single party socialist state following an Eastern European model.

A year after achieving power, the military introduced a rigid socialist system that eliminated the private business sector. All private organizations, including private schools, came under state control; the only titular private groups allowed to exist were those completely under military command.

Burma instituted autarky, and outside contacts, both ingress and egress, were eliminated as far as possible. No one legally left the country without authorization, visas for foreigners for a period were limited to twenty-four hours, internal travel was greatly restricted, and foreign and domestic news subject to complete control or censorship. Foreign missionaries who left on leave were not allowed to return. Private foreign assistance organizations were ordered to depart, and ties between internal groups and their foreign counterparts were truncated as far as possible. Burma had turned from neutral to isolationist, and an official policy of virtual xenophobia was introduced.

The BSPP through its core organization and its various subsidiary youth groups dominated all social activity. The military succeeded for the first time since independence in registering and controlling the sangha, and retail economic activity was concentrated on the cooperative sector, which was also government controlled. Professional groups were either abolished or structured along lines mandated by the center and with leadership dominated by the state and very often composed of military officers, who also controlled central and local governments. The modest autonomy enjoyed by the constituent states was eliminated at first by fiat, and then under the 1974 constitution that established a unitary state with the fiction of seven states (really provinces) organized along ethnic lines and seven divisions (also provinces) for the Burman majority.

The BSPP, controlled and in large part manned by the military, went to great lengths to mobilize public opinion and people in support of its activities. Peasants' and workers' councils were formed as further means to organize the citizenry for state purposes. Although a "feedback" mechanism was established to provide the policy makers in the *Pyuthu Hluttaw* (national assembly or legislature) with the views from the bottom of the power ladder so that the people's concerns might be taken into account, in fact it did not work. Fear of the hierarchy, which also resulted in the inflation of positive accomplishments that were politically mandated, resulted in an inadvertent avoidance of unpleasantness. While civilians feared the military, the higher officers feared those in command, and even the cabinet feared the mercurial Ne Win, and kept from him news they believed would anger him.

A few private organizations were allowed to continue—welfare and religiously oriented societies that kept far from politics or power. Those that had more than local potential were circumspect to a degree that vitiated the use of the term "civil society" in describing their activities. Advocacy groups were non-existent except for those directly mobilized by the state, or those underground or in revolt in the jungle. Dissent was publicly eliminated. Civil society had disappeared.

THE STATE LAW AND ORDER RESTORATION COUNCIL
(SLORC)

However tragic the failed revolution from below, and however destructive and bloody the repression following the coup of September 18, 1988, the military regime that came to power was simply a cosmetic change from the previous military-mandated BSPP. Although the regularization of the border trade and the openings to both the indigenous and foreign private sectors in the field of economics, and the decision to allow a multi-party political system are touted as accomplishments of the SLORC and are so reported in the internal controlled press and in the foreign popular media, this is not the case. All these changes in policy, with important and in some cases positive implications for the future, were those that had either been suggested by Ne Win at the close of his tenure as chairman of the BSPP, or had been proposed for implementation by the BSPP, but the chaos of the summer of 1988 and the coup of September intervened.

These changes were without question the most important liberalization of policies since the earlier coup of 1962. As such, they were welcomed by many. These liberalized measures should not obscure the fact that actual power had not shifted, and that it was evident from the very beginning of SLORC rule that they had no intention of reducing the ultimate control of the military over the society as a whole. What had happened was cosmetic, as we have indicated, but it was not even cosmetic surgery, but rather a thin, new patina of powder over a constant power base.

The private sector was let loose where, in national power terms, it did not threaten military rule, but in fact supported the continuation of national power under military auspices. Events have shown, and history has indicated, that the military, and indeed any conceivable civilian government in the near future, will likely be highly interventionist and not allow the market to control the economic future of the society; rather, the market mechanisms will be used within limits for economic good that will redound to both the political and economic advantage of the state and its rulers.

The center's control over non-governmental groups continued as before. It was subject to more external criticism not because it was effectively different from the repression of the BSPP era, but because the plight of Myanmar was emphasized in the international media, where there was for the first time a victim (Aung San Suu Kyi—attractive, poignant, and brave) with whom the world could identify, and during which period the times had changed for world opinion. The turmoil and killings of 1988 were not on the world's television screens live as were those of Tienanmen a year later, but world concern about the latter reinforced the former one. The presence of a large overseas Burmese expatriate community, whereas few had lived overseas in 1962, provided a convenient and dedicated base for protest. It was effectively used in many countries employing the new communications technology to organize internationally as well.

The concepts of the nature of power and its organization remained constant between the BSPP and SLORC periods. Even if those wielding it were personally different, institutionally they were the same (the military). There was no letup in the attempt to prevent the rise of any pluralistic institutions in the society that could offer avenues of public debate or disagreement over state policies and the role of the military—past, present, or future. Thus, there has been no easing of state control and as yet no indication that an autonomous civil society will be allowed to exist. There are, however, mechanisms in place that could be perceived to allow more distance between state and society. The fact that the Yangon (Rangoon) Municipality Act could be interpreted to be a "liberal" measure because under it the municipality could accept foreign assistance without going through the central authorities, something that never existed since Burma became independent, to this writer rather indicates that the military have planned a continuous hold on power at all levels and have confidence that it will continue, and thus local approval is tantamount to central approval and control.

But there have been changes in the way the state has responded to both mass mobilization and civil society. The focus of the BSPP had been on building mass mobilization organizations around the party mechanism. It became apparent in the May 1990 elections, which the government roundly lost and the results of which it continues to refuse to recognize, that there were dangers in pursuing mobilization directly through the party process. The BSPP did not work well, as the military came to realize and as we have indicated above.

To the same end of ensuring that there is a mass base for direct, vocal support for policies that the government (i.e., the military) wishes to pursue, the SLORC has taken a somewhat different route. Rather than mandating that the military and civilian personnel of the government join a party, which in the BSPP era was the only road to advancement, the SLORC moved to establish an organization called the Union Solidarity and Development Association (USDA). The founding of this organization on 15 September 1993, about two weeks after the announcement to hold a national convention to write a new constitution, is likely to be related, with the USDA as a natural and national means to disseminate support for that new law when it is finally announced.

The USDA is registered with the Ministry of Home Affairs, and is not a political party. Its explicitly mandated role is to support the activities and policies of the military, and the chairman of the SLORC is the patron. It receives both direct and indirect support from the government at various levels, although it engages in businesses to provide funds for its activities. It is not simply an "apolitical" political organization, however. It supports the state but has significant community development and educational components to attract membership. It tends to concentrate on youth, and is reported to have over five million members or some 12 percent of the population. The opposition claims that the USDA has been mobilized to protest the National League for Democracy's activities, and Aung San Suu Kyi personally, and there is no question that the activities attributed to it in the controlled press directly support state policies.[3] That the SLORC in October–November 1997 prevented Aung San Suu Kyi from personally visiting local chapters of the NLD to expand its youth activities may indicate that the SLORC is fearful of youth both as a potentially mobilized disruptive political force and that they wanted no competition with the youth activities of the USDA.

Thus, the SLORC has created its own "civil society" in the guise of the USDA. The SLORC would, and has, strongly disagreed with charges that membership is forced, but others say that there are informal, non-punitive but socially desirable incentives for joining. The potential for the USDA lies in its support for any of the SLORC policies or actions, including potentially the approval of a new constitution at some unspecified date, and the elections for a legislature that will be required. The SLORC in this case, as in many others, seems to be following the model of Indonesia, which has allowed the military to run the country for over thirty years. The USDA seems to be Golkar (the functional groups of Indonesia) before Golkar was converted from a military-sponsored social organization to a political party. The role of the military in business in Indonesia is another example of a model emulated by the Burmese military. Whether Myanmar has the institutional base on which to follow the Indonesian model is a serious question, and there are many who do not believe that Myanmar can take that route as successfully as has the Suharto government, even though General Khin Nyunt did say specifically that he admired Indonesian "stability."

There are private groups in Myanmar, but each of the several national ones, such as the Maternal and Child Welfare Association (headed by Khin Nyunt's wife) are under government influence. Other groups are cowed by the state and are clearly neither independent nor, at this stage, a force for pluralism.

Will such SLORC policies of coopting civil society continue? Probably, but even if the military remains in power through some civilianized regime in the future under a new constitution, it seems evident that pluralism will gradually expand. The stultification of state control will probably prompt private activities that will lobby for greater autonomy. The state does not have the administrative capacity to deliver the services that the population will begin to require, and burgeoning urban populations will be more difficult to administer, service, and control. The private business sector will need more space, as the state's capacity to micro-manage an economy that will become more complex will falter.

All this points to a gradual easing of the regime over time, but probably slowly and tentatively. Those who expect early change are likely to be disappointed. These changes may come about inadvertently rather than through conscious policy decisions. There is always the possibility of a counter-military coup, or a popular uprising, but both seem unlikely at this writing. We are, therefore, likely to witness the gradual erosion of military ubiquity, but not basic power in areas that it regards as of national importance. The military's views of security extend far and wide. It is unlikely to change soon.

We should not place faith that the change on 15 November 1997 of the name of the ruling coalition of military from SLORC to SPDC (State Peace and Development Council) means a change in policy. This is likely a tactical move to ameliorate a poor international image, for the leadership at the apex of the council remains the same, and there is still no civilian element in its operation. Thus the immediate future for civil society remains bleak

NOTES

1. The State Law and Order Restoration Council changed the name of the country from Burma to Myanmar in 1989, and has insisted on its use for all periods and in all grammatical forms. This has become a political issue, as it is not accepted by the opposition, and is thus an indicator of political orientation. Here the terms are used without political intent: Myanmar for the period under SLORC, Burma for the previous periods, Burmese as an adjective, and Burman to indicate the major ethnic group in the country.

2. See J. S. Furnivall, *Colonial Policies and Practice. A Comparative Study of Burma and Netherlands India.* Cambridge: Cambridge University Press, 1957.

3. See David I. Steinberg, "Mobilization and Orthodoxy in Myanmar: The Union Solidarity and Development Association." *Burma Debate*, Spring 1997.

ETHNIC CONFLICT AND THE CHALLENGE OF CIVIL SOCIETY IN BURMA

MARTIN SMITH

OVERVIEW: THE CHANGING POLITICAL CONTEXT AND DILEMMA OF ENGAGEMENT

The peaceful and lasting solution to the long-running ethnic conflicts in Burma is, without doubt, one of the most integral challenges facing the country today. Indeed, it cannot be separated from the greater challenges of social, political, and economic reform in the country at large. Since the seismic events of 1988, Burma has remained deadlocked in its third critical period of political and social transition since independence in 1948. However, despite the surface impasse, the political landscape has not remained static. During the past decade, the evidence of desire for fundamental political change has spread to virtually every sector of society, and, at different stages, this desire for change has been articulated by representatives of all the major political, ethnic, military and social organizations or factions. That Burma, therefore, has entered an era of enormous political volatility and transformation is not in dispute.

Serious doubts, of course, continue to dog how and when any reform process will be brought about to the satisfaction of all Burma's long-suffering peoples—and this remains a central dilemma for international non-governmental organizations (NGOs). But for those looking to the long term and hoping for peaceful change, it is significant that, since 1988, the new political climate has been reflected in a number of initiatives, which—in one way or another—have engaged all the key protagonists. Military rule still predominates but, despite the lack of consensual progress, the very nature of these exchanges or contacts marks a notable change in the pattern in Burmese politics from the *Burmese Way to Socialism* era of General Ne Win that preceded it. Equally important as further evidence of the changes underway, the door has also been opened to a growing cast of international organizations and actors who have also begun to engage with different elements and communities within broader Burmese society. All such developments were virtually unthinkable just a decade ago.

By contrast, during a quarter century of Ne Win's isolationist rule (1962–88), national political and economic life had ossified and, in many respects, could be separated into two different—although overlapping—socio-political arenas: firstly, the Dry Zone, Irrawaddy plains and other lowland areas where the Burman majority mostly live; and, secondly, the ethnic minority borderlands.

In the major towns and Burman heartland, Ne Win's military-backed Burma Socialist Program Party (BSPP) attempted to build up a monolithic system of government which would, it was intended, radiate out from Rangoon into the ethnic minority states. Meanwhile, in the deep mountains and forests of the borderland periphery, over twenty armed opposition groups controlled, under their own administrations, vast swathes of territory and continued to reflect an often changing alignment of different political or nationality causes. Simplifications can be made here, too, for although the politics often appeared complicated, most such groups espoused just one of two major ideologies—either communism or federalism based on a loosely Western democratic model.[1]

The BSPP was to collapse almost without trace during the pro-democracy protests in 1988, but Ne Win loyalists reasserted military control through the takeover of the State Law and Order Restoration Council (SLORC) in September that year. This triggered one of the periodic but complex periods of shakeup and realignment in Burmese politics, which also saw the emergence of Daw Aung San Suu Kyi's National League for Democracy (NLD). The result is a pattern of political and social transformation that is still continuing. More recently, for example, the SLORC restructured the military government to reemerge in November 1997 as the State Peace and Development Council (SPDC), while in mid-1998 the NLD began a publicity campaign to be allowed to form a new parliament in an effort to resolve the political deadlock within the country.

The political impasse thus remains, but what is immediately striking in the post-1988 scenario is that, on paper at least, the end goals of the leading actors and parties for the first time appear remarkably similar. As in many other countries around the world, much of the ideological dogma of the cold war era has been abandoned. Instead, although few issues have been mutually broached, all parties profess to support change to a "market-oriented," "open-door," "multi-party" system of "democratic" government, all of which are elements that are generally considered essential building blocks in the development of civil society. Furthermore, in apparent acknowledgment of the failures of the past, all sides have pledged to pay greater attention, in Burma's future constitution, to the political, cultural, economic, and social rights of Burma's ethnic minority peoples, who make up an estimated third of the country's 48 million population.

In reality, of course, many observers would argue that, whatever the rhetoric, the real struggle in Burmese politics over the past decade has been for control of the transitional process—and this has yet to be resolved. In particular, it is frequently noted how, during this period of deadlock, the Burmese armed forces have only continued to grow and increase domination over many aspects of daily life.[2] To concentrate on this alone, however, would be to underestimate just how much the internal political context and structures have been changing within Burma. A titanic battle of wills is underway in which all sides, through different tactics and exchanges, have been attempting to put their views on to center stage.

As evidence of such changes, two events stand out: the 1990 general election and the ethnic ceasefire movement in the country's borderlands. In the former case, the election, which was organized by the military government, was overwhelmingly won by the NLD with 82 percent of the seats; strikingly, too, not only did ethnic minority voters support the NLD in many parts of the country, but candidates from nineteen different ethnic minority parties won the second largest block of constituencies. Subsequently, the SLORC, proclaiming the duty of "national politics," announced a hand-picked National Convention, consisting of representatives from eight "social" categories (including MPS), to actually draw up the new constitution, but, in the eyes of most of the world, a clear marker of democratic hopes and intent had already been laid by Burma's peoples through the election result.[3]

In actually recharting the socio-political environment in the field, however, the second development has been equally significant: the ceasefire movement in the ethnic minority war zones. Here there were no central government elections, but, also instituted by the SLORC, this movement spread during the 1990s to include the majority of armed ethnic opposition groups in Burma (see appendix). Indeed, in tandem with the government's "open-door" shift to a market-oriented economy, the very existence of these ceasefires has marked a major change in the political and social context of daily life and relationships in many parts of the country. In fact, not only was the NLD, which has been subject to many obstructions, barred from the National Convention after a series of disagreements with the SLORC in 1995, but representatives of several ceasefire parties have, by contrast, actually been continuing to attend.

In examining recent history, then, this much is easy to document and analyze. But adjudging where such developments will lead Burma and its different nationality peoples on their road to social and political progress, let alone the modern concept of "civil society," is a very different and infinitely more difficult task. This is not only a dilemma within Burma. In the international community, too, there remain continuing disagreements over whether such goals as social progress, human rights, economic advancement, and human or sustainable development—all of which are considered the bedrock of civil society—can really be achieved until there is, first, substantive political reform.

Recent experiences, for example, in South Africa, Eastern Europe, or Indonesia all provide important models for comparison. But in the final analysis, experience the world over has demonstrated that much has hinged on the actions of the peoples and protagonists themselves. There is, as such, no prescriptive model. As David Steinberg has written: "Clearly in the polarization between isolation or engagement, investment or abstention, both poles can be 'correct.'"[4]

Such differences of opinion over social and political priorities are already having a critical impact within Burma. For example, while

Burma's oldest armed ethnic opposition group, the Karen National Union (KNU), has consistently argued against any ceasefire without a political agreement (which, in part, again resulted in fierce fighting with the Burmese armed forces in southeast Burma during 1997), other armed ethnic opposition groups, including former KNU allies such as the Pao National Organization (PNO) and Kachin Independence Organization (KIO), have decided to place ceasefires and the establishment of "peace through development" first. After decades of inconclusive warfare, not only do such groups regard development and social welfare as the initial priority for their peoples, but they also believe (or trust) that such peace will eventually prove the foundation for reconciliation and reform.[5]

Similar contradictions also exist on the economic front, which is usually regarded as another main element in the development of civil society in any democracy. For example, while Daw Suu Kyi and the NLD have argued in support of international trading boycotts until there is substantive political reform, the state-controlled media has repeatedly denounced the NLD for allegedly holding up the progress of the nation through its tactics and goals.[6]

Inevitably, such a debate also embroils foreign governments, companies and development agencies, and this division of opinion is already marked in a number of ethnic minority areas, notably in the Tenasserim Division in southernmost Burma. Here the KNU has opposed the construction through Karen-inhabited areas of the Yadana gas pipeline, which is a joint venture between Total (France), Unocal (USA), PTTEP (Thailand) and the state-owned Myanma Oil and Gas Enterprise. In response, Total claims to have embarked on over US$ 6 million of "socio-economic initiatives," including health and development programs, with the aim of increasing community "self-sufficiency"—and with respect for local "customs" and "culture."[7] Indeed, not only is the pipeline Burma's single largest foreign investment project, but, save for the UNHCR's very different resettlement program for Muslim refugees in the Rakhine state, Total's community programs are probably the single largest such "integrated" development venture in any minority-inhabited region today. In a once forgotten corner of Burma, the long-term implications are immense.

REALITIES ON THE GROUND: WEAK STATE AND STRONG SOCIETIES

The entrance, then, of foreign agencies—whether inter-governmental, non-governmental or business—raises further difficult questions over priorities in reform and development, especially where the notion of "civil society" is concerned. Historically, the timing is striking, and Burma is certainly not alone. For as Mark Duffield and other public policy academics have noted, since the ending of the cold war there has been an explosion of interest and involvement by inter-governmental and non-governmental organizations (mostly Western) in "conflict resolution" in divided countries or societies. Here, while "dialogue" is usually encouraged on protagonists, the primacy of development and humanitarian relief are often principally involved, and it is often for such reasons of "crisis" or "need" that different international agencies have first become engaged.

Once again, however, as recent experiences from Rwanda to Cambodia have shown, there is nothing prescriptive about such measures. The simplistic divisions of the international community during the cold war may be disappearing along with polarized models for national development, but the new result is very often a great deal of individual agenda-setting by different international organizations, where the perspectives and language brought to bear on problems can say more about the different organizations than the actual situation on the ground in the various troublespots around the world. In such countries of crisis, questions of humanitarian relief, aid, or human rights, including the right to life and the right to development, frequently have to compete alongside new buzzwords, such as "complex emergencies," "corridors of peace," "culture of dependency," "human development," or more recently, "Asian values." In short, different international organizations with different remits may well find themselves working on different sides—or through different institutions or protagonists in a conflict. Such is frequently the case in Burma today.

It is to reconcile such obvious differences that the subject of "civil society" has most recently been brought in. But as Mark Duffield has warned:

In both development and transitional thinking, civil society has become a central concept. This development is all the more interesting given the absence among aid agencies and donor governments of any consensus regarding what civil society is and how it works. At best, it is an ill-defined space between the family and state in which plural civic institutions hold sway.[8]

The debate is still continuing, but, amongst international agencies, two trends or mooted solutions are becoming clear. In the humanitarian or development world, emphasis is placed on the working practices of agencies themselves, including working at the "grassroots" level wherever possible (if feasible, through local partnerships), with such long-term aims as "capacity building," "social mobilization," "participatory planning," and community "enhancement" or "empowerment." In effect, while avoiding political alignment with the state alone, agencies are trying to work within the presumed space that Duffield has described. Information sharing, too, with other agencies is also desired so that the broader picture of needs can be kept in view. And, in many respects, these are the patterns of engagement which are already developing for agencies working in or around Burma. Indeed, pressure for such practices underpinned the exceptional decision, in May 1992, of the Governing Council of the United Nations Development Program (UNDP) to begin a review of its country program so that future projects would be limited to critical humanitarian and "basic human development initiatives" at the "grass-roots level."[9]

These, then, are the kind of working practices that international agencies have already evolved. But many recipients and observers are becoming concerned that, devoid of socio-political context, such practices are not enough. As a result, a second trend of analysis, highly relevant to Burma, is also emerging amongst aid workers and political scientists, who have become frustrated at the seeming inability of the international community to achieve positive results—despite generally good intentions—in many of the more intractable crisis regions of the world. Recently outstanding in this respect have been several countries in the Balkans and Central Africa, where locals and more knowledgeable observers have decried the international tendency to overlook the local dynamics or causes of conflict and suffering, which may be very individual, but to loosely generalize in a language of "emergency" and "chaos," where the agendas are too often simplified by aid agencies or driven by media headlines.

Instead, a number of observers now argue that the first priority should be to look at institutional and social problems from the ground up, by focusing attention on the diverse peoples who live in such countries and by gaining a greater appreciation of the depth and vibrancy of their cultures, as well as their problems, as they exist in the field. Perhaps not surprisingly, immediately paramount in such a "ground-up" analysis are usually two common features—ethnic conflict and the weakness of the state—which, although complex, have to be individually confronted according to the circumstances in each country. This, of course, is very easy to say; but as John Ryle, Save the Children Fund consultant for Africa, has recently warned those looking for simple solutions: "Each of these conflicts emerges from a particular history in which the pattern of colonial heritage, community politics and state formation or non-formation is quite distinct . . . . generalizations are dangerous."[10]

So, are there any lessons in this for international NGOs with a working interest in Burma? Certainly, there are—especially in ethnic minority areas and for those proponents of civil society who support the notion of institutional pluralism, human rights, and community bridge-building as ways to encourage and stabilize reform. The correlation between the development of civil society, on the one hand, and the role of different political, social, governmental, religious, or economic institutions, on the other hand, is hardly an exact science. But beyond the day-to-day headlines, as John Ryle has explained, there usually lies a historic malfunctioning between the development of equitable state and local community relations. Again, such has long been the case in Burma.

Thus, away from theoretical models, any discussion of civil society in Burma has to take cognizance, at some stage, of the ethnic and political realities on the ground. Moreover, given the scale of conflict and bloodshed in the past five decades, it needs to be recognized that reform and social transformation are long-term processes and will undoubtedly remain a challenge for any government that comes to power in Rangoon in the coming years. Many areas of Burma today are suffering a devastating social legacy from the armed conflicts and destruction that have continued, virtually uninterrupted, since independence in 1948.

Therefore, in this overview it is important to highlight, from the perspective of civil society, some of the particular problems and characteristics in the deep socio-political crisis that has developed in Burma. For while it is generally true to say that in the past decade, Burmese politics have come to be dominated by three key blocks—the Burmese armed forces or *Tatmadaw*, the fledgling democracy movement headed by Daw Suu Kyi, and the diverse armed ethnic opposition groups—such distinctions should not be regarded as absolute divisions, and especially not where the development of civil society is contemplated.

In recent years, for example, the United Nations General Assembly has repeatedly supported the call for "tri-partite" dialogue as a pragmatic first step out of the current impasse. But this does not then mean that democracy cannot also be a main aspiration of the *Tatmadaw* or the ethnic nationality opposition nor that there can be no ethnic minority representatives in the *Tatmadaw* or NLD. Indeed, from the perspective of civil society, the very reverse should be true; as civil society develops in Burma, if democratic institutions and practices are to take root and survive, all the many different social, ethnic, and political factions or institutions in this most ethnically diverse of countries will have to respect and share common values. All sectors of society must be engaged, including the *Tatmadaw*. As Chao Tzang Yawnghwe, a political scientist and former Shan armed opposition leader, recently wrote:

> Top generals will have to learn how to deal with military pluralism and, by extension, with societal pluralism. What Burma needs is not political order by command, but by negotiation, accommodation and bargaining between and among all segments, groups and sectors in society.[11]

Similarly, where ethnic minority communities are concerned, the short-hand division between "black" (insurgent-controlled), "brown" (no-man's land) and "white" (government-controlled) will have to be abandoned. Inhabiting up to half the land area, minority communities are not marginal; they are an inseparable part of Burma's ethnic mosaic. Indeed, few large regions of the country can be considered truly mono-ethnic. Current battle-lines or ethnic designations of territory, therefore, cannot be regarded as definitive where the development of civil society is concerned—and certainly not in socio-political areas such as humanitarian relief, education, or the provision of basic healthcare.

Nearly 200,000 Shans, for example, are estimated to live in the Kachin state, while over 100,000 Kachins live in the Shan state.[12] In the Shan state, in particular, there exists one of the most complicated ethnic and insurgency situations in the world. Well into the last decade of the twentieth century, over a dozen armed ethnic opposition groups have continued to control different areas of the state, from where they still vie for authority with the central government in Rangoon.

It is important to remember, therefore, that, as elsewhere in the country, it is to this backdrop of unresolved conflict that many of the grave issues have arisen which so concern the international community today, including extrajudicial killings, forced relocations, the opium trade, and more recently, the rapid spread of HIV/AIDS. Such human rights abuses or social crises do not occur in a vacuum.

In conclusion, then, when looking at the complex scale of problems Burma is facing, it is important to stress, in any analysis, the underlying weaknesses of the modern Burmese state and, fifty years after independence, its historic role in generating rather than healing social and ethnic divisions. In this respect, Burma bears many of the characteristics of the phenomenon, much commented on in recent years, known as "strong societies" and "weak state," where post-colonial governments have been unable to achieve—or countenance—effective action across all social and ethnic sectors. (This, of course, does not reflect "military power," which the Burmese armed forces clearly possess.)

In the post-colonial world, Burma is hardly alone in facing such an experience, but what is immediately striking in Burma's case is both the predominant role of military organizations (of various colors) in national life as well as the strong ethnic undercurrents in political and social movements. Indeed, in many respects, ethnicity is an ideology in Burma, which has frequently been described by the country's military rulers as the "Yugoslavia of Asia"; this, they claim, would similarly fall apart without their eternal vigilance. In response, minority organizations accuse the mostly Burman leaders of the *Tatmadaw* of using such pretexts as a guise to try and create an "ethnocratic" Burman state under their sole control.

Thus, in another time of transformation, the question must be addressed as to why, in the past five decades, Burma has had so little success in addressing problems of post-colonial transition. In a land as ethnically diverse as Burma, of course, the local imperative or perception can never be underestimated in understanding local community or ethnic organization and reaction, but, by any standards, the history of the modern Burmese state is an unhappy one. Yet, in contrast, many different societies in Burma have successfully continued to adapt and survive through the many difficult years. By every criteria of such political scientists as Barry Buzan and David Brown, the evidence of strong societies in Burma—whether ethnic (e.g. Shan, Mon, Karen), religious (Buddhist, Christian, or Muslim), minority nationalist (KNU, KIO) or even business (Chinese, Indian)—stands in stark contrast to the structural weaknesses of the state which, even in the late twentieth century, has still not effectively penetrated into many ethnic minority regions, except as a military force.

As Barry Buzan has written: "Weak states either do not have, or have failed to create, a domestic political and social consensus of sufficient strength to eliminate the large-scale use of force as a major and continuing element in the domestic political life of the nation."[13]

The key issue, then, remains as to whether the recent actions taken by the leading political protagonists in Burma—and indeed, the notions of civil society—will create the space needed for real "domestic political and social consensus" to emerge. For it is in this complex environment that international NGOs have recently become engaged in Burma and the ethnic minority borderlands.

CEASEFIRES AND RECENT EVENTS IN ETHNIC MINORITY REGIONS

It is with such perspectives in mind, of a post-colonial state in internal conflict and crisis, that recent events in ethnic minority areas of Burma need to be regarded. From one region of the country to another, while general health or social characteristics may often be constant, the actual situation or tensions on the ground can be significantly different. This may be as much due to local protagonists, institutions or parties as to social factors, such as the opium trade, the continuing movement (and displacement) of peoples or the current state of fighting.

This presents an immediate dilemma for international organizations entering such long-divided regions. For, at such a time of transition, it is by no means clear which parties or institutions will develop and grow—and which institutions, in contrast, will stumble and fall. The Union Solidarity and Development Association (USDA), for example, which is increasingly the military government's preferred vehicle for social and political action, was formed as recently as September 1993 but, with government patronage, has already grown to several million members. Similarly, while the once powerful Communist Party of Burma (CPB) has collapsed, Burma's strongest armed opposition force, the United Wa State Party (UWSP), was only formed in 1989 but has over 20,000 well-armed troops today.

Finally, in ethnic minority regions the human dimension can never be ignored. In many areas, decades of war, human rights' abuses and confrontation have created a climate where nothing is ever certain, as many citizens have found to their cost. The desire for peaceful change may be widespread across the country, but the fact is that, for the moment, fear, opportunism, or survival have all too often been the key motivations for action rather than reconciliation and reform, which will require long-term thinking and support.

To follow the ceasefires, then, a great deal of history needs to be condensed. The peace movement, in fact, began almost by chance in northeast Burma in 1989, following a series of ethnic mutinies from the CPB, which was, at the time, Burma's oldest and largest insurgent force. During 1980–81, under the former BSPP government, there had been peace talks between the government and CPB as well as with the Kachin Independence Organization (KIO) in northeast Burma, but the last major round of countrywide peace talks had, in fact, been as long ago as 1963–64, shortly after General Ne Win assumed power. In the long years since, despite the perennial strength and extensive "liberated zones" of insurgent forces, the possibility of further peace talks was consistently ruled out by the central government which, instead, described armed opposition groups by such terms as "bandits," "opium smugglers," or "racist saboteurs," who were only to be "annihilated."[14]

By the end of the 1980s, however, the mood was very different—especially after fierce fighting broke out following the SLORC's assumption of power in September 1988. Armed opposition movements had been noticeably quiet during the dramatic events that swept the country in mid-1988. This was partly due to their remoteness (the pro-democracy protests were largely urban-based), but it was also by design; both ethnic and communist leaders had warned of the dangers of trying to exploit the Burmese army's difficulties during such a time of political awakening.

The subsequent arrival of an estimated 10,000 students and other democracy activists (most of whom were ethnic Burmans) seeking sanctuary in armed opposition territory after the SLORC takeover, only acted as further confirmation of the changing political landscape. However, to the anguish of leaders and communities on all sides, over a thousand lives were lost in the bloody battles that erupted, especially in KNU-, KIO- and CPB-controlled territory where many democracy activists had fled. While central Burma was in crisis (and the democracy movement was newly emergent), it was therefore in ethnic minority regions that the greatest violence had now transferred.[15]

Clearly, all sides—including the Burmese armed forces and the ethnic minority opposition—had their own reasons for now considering ceasefires, and these were to subsequently come from two major blocks: those of former allies or defectors from the CPB, many of which still support the establishment of "autonomous zones" along the model of China, or members of the eleven-party National Democratic Front (NDF) established in 1976, which has long advocated the formation of a federal union of Burma.

The first to make ceasefires were five (subsequently four) breakaway armies from the CPB, spearheaded by the United Wa State Party in eastern Shan State, all of which agreed truces during 1989. Correctly sensing their unwillingness to fight on at such an uncertain time,[16] the initial approaches had been made by Lt-Gen. Khin Nyunt, the SLORC secretary-one and military intelligence chief. However, little-noticed, the socio-political sub-text was already changing, and an important go-between role was played by the former insurgent leader and now powerful businessman, Lo Hsing-han, who was able to liaise and convince local kinsmen of the claimed possibilities for peace and development in the Kokang region, where the first CPB mutinies had occurred.

Equally important, despite a series of approaches from NDF members, the CPB mutineers rejected advances from other political groups and organizations. Indeed, in September 1989, the main wing of an important NDF member, the Shan State Progress Party, which had been close to the CPB in northern Shan State, also made a ceasefire agreement. It was a timely reminder of the historic lack of unity amongst what is loosely described as the "ethnic opposition."

The fallout, then, from these first ceasefires was to set in train a number of unpredicted consequences. Whether by design or not, one of the most significant was the newly "legalized" nexus between the Burmese armed forces, armed ethnic opposition groups, business interests, governmental institutions, and, ultimately, local community groups. This was to set a precedent for future ceasefires as well as fundamentally change the basis of the economy in many border regions. Previously, under the *Burmese Way to Socialism*, much of the local trade was insurgent-controlled, and there was a flourishing trade in everything from cattle, precious stones, and opium to luxury goods and medicines.

Now, however, for the first time in decades, the pattern was set for all legal trading relationships in the border regions to be brought "inside" the country. From the frontier with Bangladesh to the borders with Thailand, gaining control of land (or, at least, a physical presence) has become a key priority of the post-1988 military government, and four additional regional commands were established in border areas in 1996.

This has had the most profound consequences, both at home and abroad. Firstly, with border regions increasingly within its ambit, the SLORC/SPDC government has been able to build on its intention to end Burma's international isolation and formalize official trading and political relations with its different neighbors. Neighboring governments have also positively responded, especially China and Thailand, which had previously tolerated (or even quietly supported) armed opposition groups along their borders. Burma's admission into ASEAN in July 1997 is only the most obvious manifestation of such a change.

However, secondly, and equally important from the perspective of civil society, in the past eight years the central government has been slowly "legitimizing" or allowing new economic, political, and social networks, which have been slowly coming to life inside all the ethnic minority borderlands. The permission, for example, for both UN agencies and international NGOs to visit or even work in these once forbidden areas is simply another example of these broader changes, which would scarcely have been feasible without ceasefires and the new perspectives from Rangoon.

At this stage, it should be stressed that, back in 1989, only the most rudimentary agreements were made and, in effect, there were no political discussions at all. For example, it was agreed that in this transitional period under the SLORC, the ceasefire forces would be allowed to keep their arms and territory until Burma's new constitution was introduced. But these were deliberately skeletal terms which, perhaps because of their simplicity, satisfied both sides. Nevertheless, further details were also discussed, including the government's introduction of health and development programs in ethnic minority areas. Notably, as early as May 1989, the SLORC's much-publicized Border Areas Development Program (BADP) was first announced, with eight to ten million inhabitants, in fourteen different minority regions, predicted to come under its mandate.[17]

As an interim measure, varying subsidies and supplies were also donated by the government until the different forces could become self-sufficient. In this regard, the complex question of opium production, which is the main cash crop in some of these areas, was also discussed. Although different protagonists have subsequently disagreed over specifics, it was mutually agreed to take a long-term view on the problem of abolition and, instead, work on a ten-year program involving the help of UN agencies, to phase in different crop substitution projects. This, of course, has subsequently become one of the most critical areas of international concern, attracting particular criticism from governments in the West which have recognized that in some areas, opium production has, in contrast, continued to rise.[18]

In effect, then, the five main ceasefire agreements in 1989 set a precedent for the further ceasefires which were to come in later years. Equally important, although there have been frequent predictions of breakdown, all five have, to date, survived through the decade since, despite a plethora of obvious day-to-day difficulties. Moreover, the very existence of these ceasefires along the China border has had an immediate impact on armed opposition movements elsewhere in the country.

In strategic terms, the first impact was felt by insurgent organizations in adjoining areas. These, for the first time, came under enormous pressures not only from their own peoples to consider ceasefires but also from the Burmese army, which no longer had to guard its rear. Once again, subsequent events were to reveal a new mood in the country—this time within the National Democratic Front.

After 1988, recognizing the unpredictable environment, a number of NDF groups had also privately argued for the proposal of peace talks, notably the late KIO chairman, Maran Brang Seng, and the PNO chairman, Aung Kham Hti. Other NDF members, however, and most especially the Karen National Union, were keen to concentrate on the expansion of armed opposition forces in Burma's borderlands, particularly through the formation of the Democratic Alliance of Burma (DAB), which included student, trade union, Buddhist, and other pro-democracy groups that had sprung up during the anti-government protests in 1988. Subsequently, another well-publicized front, the National Council Union of Burma (NCUB), was also set up, which joined with the DAB and the National Coalition Government Union of Burma (NCGUB), consisting of a dozen MPs (mostly NLD) who had won seats in the 1990 election.

Such developments, however, while well reported in the international media, failed to develop beyond border politics and had limited impact on the actual state of the conflict inside the country. Indeed, not only were many minority inhabitants unaware of such movements, but many minority leaders and communities in urban areas were rather more focused on the implications of the 1990 general election in which ethnic nationalist parties, after over a quarter century of banishment, were now "legally" allowed to stand.

Thus, with the NDF and DAB both hesitating, the Burmese army was quick to sense this vacuum. Although leaving the door to peace talks open, during 1990-91 the army launched sustained military offensives in northeast Burma, especially in Pao, Shan, Palaung and Kachin-inhabited areas, in which hundreds of villages were relocated or destroyed. Other military operations were also launched in northwest Burma which fueled the gathering exodus of over 250,000 Muslim refugees from the Rakhine state into Bangladesh. Despite its severity, this "stick and carrot" approach appeared to work, providing the backdrop to a succession of ceasefires by NDF forces in early 1991—

firstly by the KIO's 4th Brigade in northern Shan state (which defected from the KIO to establish a new "Kachin Defense Army") and then the Pao National Organization and the Palaung State Liberation Party in quick succession afterwards.

By early 1992, therefore, the socio-political landscape in ethnic minority regions was rapidly changing. Military rule continued, but the 1990 election result had signified a massive victory for the NLD and ethnic minority parties, most of whom were allied in the United Nationalities League for Democracy which was supported by sixty-five MPs. Already open contacts had been established between some of the victorious political parties and ceasefire armies that had opened business and liaison offices in the towns. In addition, although controversial, the Border Areas Development Program was now well underway, and, for the first time in decades representatives of several UN agencies (especially UNDP, UNDCP, and UNICEF) were being allowed into a number of districts in the long-forbidden hills.

Quietly, too, the SLORC was preparing for the National Convention, which was to draw up the principles for Burma's new constitution, the country's third since independence. A number of government officials initially thought that as a counter-balance to the NLD, they might be able to foster the support of different ethnic nationality parties—both ceasefire groups and those that had stood in the election; this, however, was not to work out exactly as planned.[19]

To try, then, to accelerate the ceasefire process, in April 1992 the SLORC unexpectedly announced that the Burmese army was halting all offensive operations against armed ethnic opposition groups in "the name of national unity." This followed hundreds of casualties on both sides in one of the most publicized battles ever in the history of the country's long insurgencies: the unsuccessful offensive to capture the joint KNU/DAB headquarters at Mannerplaw. Subsequently, the Burmese army did remain on front-line patrol and sporadic fighting occurred, but, in many areas, the levels of day-to-day violence dropped to their lowest levels in decades. Indeed, as another warning of the unpredictability of ethnic conflict in Burma, it was in two new areas that most of the new violence was reported: in the Rakhine state, where fallout from the flight of the Muslim refugees was still continuing, and in the southern Shan state, where the 15,000-strong Mong Tai Army of the "opium kingpin" Khun Sa was isolated and briefly went on the offensive.

Subsequent events are still the subject of much conjecture, as the remaining NDF parties failed to agree on any concrete platform or strategy towards peace talks. Many veteran leaders recognized that the SLORC's 1992 announcement was significant, since it laid the negotiating basis for a "nationwide ceasefire," something that they had themselves long advocated. In reality, however, the situation was very different from one ethnic nationality area to another, and this owed much to the different strengths and supporters of the different parties and armed forces, as well as the different sentiments in the local communities.

Probably the most effective and united movement towards a ceasefire occurred in northeast Burma, where leaders of the Kachin Independence Organization had long argued for dialogue and a peaceful solution to the civil war; the dilemma had always been over how to bring this about. Significantly, too, as in 1980–81, the peace movement here was under-pinned by a cross-community approach in which church groups and leading Kachin figures in government-controlled areas were also involved. Thus, not only were such organizations and intermediaries able to play an important "go-between" role, but the question of peace was not simply a topic of debate between the Burmese army and KIO; the discussions were also keenly followed in other sectors of Kachin society, including in the towns and villages and amongst business people and government servants.

In many ways, then, the depth of this prior discussion has probably reflected the greater energy behind the ceasefire movement in Kachin areas where, despite many cautions, perhaps the widest array of humanitarian, development, and educational projects has been initiated following the 1994 military truce. Here a particular concern was the feeling that, while the KIO and Kachin people continued the political fight, other ethnic groups, especially Chinese, were coming in to take over business and trade under the SLORC's "open door" policy.

Other ethnic nationality forces based around the Thai border, however, were not so convinced, and when in 1993 the SLORC said that it was prepared to meet a joint delegation of Kachin, Mon, Karenni, and Karen members of the NDF, the different opposition groups could not unite on tactics. Thus in February 1994, following its expulsion from the DAB, the KIO, which was probably the NDF's strongest force, became the next armed opposition group to agree a ceasefire with the SLORC.

Once again, a ceasefire in northeast Burma was to have a major impact on the military-political balance elsewhere. Not only did the remaining armed opposition forces now begin to hear doubts from amongst their own peoples, but those in the Thai border area began to come under serious pressures from the authorities in Thailand which, by this stage, was wanting to admit Burma into ASEAN. With growing numbers of refugees (around 100,000) and illegal migrants (over 500,000) from Burma, many Thai officers openly questioned why local ethnic minority forces in southeast Burma, unlike the UWSP or KIO in the northeast, could not agree ceasefires with the Burmese government.

After decades of being regarded as "buffer zones" by the Thai authorities, the armed ethnic opposition was thus for the first time being seen as a hindrance to peace and development in the region. Here the new talk was of trade, commerce, infrastructure building, and power generation that crossed international frontiers. Already, despite the objections of opposition voices, unbridled trades in logging and fishing had developed between new military-backed business networks emerging on both sides. In southeast Burma, armed opposition groups were now under threat of being bypassed altogether.

At this critical moment, the credibility of the KNU took a severe blow when several hundred Buddhist Karen troops, led by a local abbot, broke away to agree a ceasefire with the SLORC and set up the rival Democratic Karen Buddhist Army in the Paan area. Their initial allegation was of anti-Buddhist discrimination by some of the KNU's predominantly Christian leaders (most Karens are, in fact, Buddhists), but the end result has been the loss of the KNU headquarters at Mannerplaw and a desultory campaign of inter-Karen conflict which, to the concern of the international community, has also seen the DKBA attack and burn down a number of Karen refugee camps in Thailand.

Thus, in 1994–95, the ceasefire movement began to gather momentum again, although this time the different ethnic minority forces were rather more reluctant and cautious. Nonetheless, a number of ceasefires were quickly agreed, including by the Kayan New Land Party, Karenni State Nationalities Liberation Front and Shan State

Nationalities Liberation Organization, all of which had previously been close to the CPB, and by the New Mon State Party (NMSP) and Karenni National Progressive Party (KNPP), which were Thai border–based members of the NDF (see appendix). Unlike the Kachin case, however, broad-based and effective liaison between these groups and the military government presented a problem—except in some of the predominantly Christian communities in the Kayah-Shan state borderlands, where an important "go-between" role was again played by local church officials.

The SLORC also received an added bonus in January 1996 when the maverick Shan-Chinese leader Khun Sa virtually delivered his Mong Tai Army (MTA) over to the Burmese army in a surprise ceremony at his headquarters at Homong in southwest Shan state. This many Shan nationalists saw as more of a surrender than ceasefire between military equals, and it was widely recalled that, like the Kokang leader Lo Hsing-han, Khun Sa had twice served in the 1960s and 70s as a local "Ka Kwe Ye" militia commander on the government side. Indeed Khun Sa, like Lo Hsing-han, had also served time in government prisons; the little-admitted fact is that, in the complex twists and turns of Burma's insurgent world, at the front there are commanders who have always played both sides.[20] By now, however, there was little time for analysis: ceasefires were becoming commonplace around the country—and being made on a variety of very different terms.

The KNU, too, which was now badly weakened by the DKBA split, also became engaged in a protracted series of peace negotiations during 1995–96. These, however, broke down at the end of the year when the KNU, sticking to its long-time demand for a "political settlement first," rejected two government demands: that the KNU "enter the legal fold" and renounce the "right to armed struggle." Subsequently, in early 1997 the KNU's Seventh Day Adventist chairman, Bo Mya, hosted a much-publicized Ethnic Nationalities Seminar at the village of Mae Tha Raw Hta where the participants issued a declaration in which the KNU announced, amongst other things, its support for Aung San Suu Kyi and the NLD and its intention to bring down the military government.

Few observers, then, were surprised when fighting quickly resumed, but, with the KNU now weakened by surrenders and defections, few predicted the speed of the Burmese army break-through. During 1997, remaining KNU base areas fell one after another. Once again, however, the main victims have been the villagers caught in the cross-fire, with over 20,000 new refugees attempting to flee into Thailand, where the authorities have recently begun to try and forcibly prevent any more people trying to cross. But the plight of civilians is undoubtedly worse back in the war zones in Burma. Tragically, after five decades of armed conflict, local community leaders estimate that in the Karen state alone as many as one third of the one million plus inhabitants are now displaced from their homes—either in refugee camps or exile in Thailand, internally displaced in the hills, or forced to move into the towns or government-controlled settlements. Peace, reform, reconciliation, and the creation of civil society in such a divided community is, for the moment, clearly an imponderable task.

Thus, in conclusion, depending on where one is standing, a number of very different perspectives can be taken on the current situation in ethnic minority regions of Burma. The fighting in several Karen-inhabited districts of southeast Burma can be contrasted with the durability, to date, of the ceasefires and hopes for development in Kachin, Palaung, Pao and Wa communities in the northeast. In the Rakhine state, too, the resettlement under UNHCR auspices of over 200,000 Muslim refugees from Bangladesh can be contrasted with the anti-Muslim violence that swept a number of towns across the country earlier in the year—and, indeed, reportedly reached the Rakhine state again.

A number of the more recent ceasefires have also proven unstable. In 1995, the ceasefire of the Karenni National Progressive Party quickly broke down, following unreconciled disagreements over territory and trade, while, more recently, there have been reports of clashes between Burmese army units and the Kayan New Land Party. Equally serious, major fighting has resumed in southwest and central Shan state where a veteran nationalist faction, the Shan United Revolutionary Army, has rejected the terms of Khun Sa's MTA surrender and is attempting to resume the Shan resistance. According to the UN Special Rapporteur on Human Rights, as a consequence of these conflicts, over seven hundred villages have been relocated in the Shan and Kayah state borderlands in the past two years alone.[21] Completing this picture of confusion (and leaving aside the politics of Rangoon), there have also been a number of local splits amongst different opposition militia, including Kokang, Mon, Karen and Shan, which are too numerous to mention.

Nevertheless, despite this present picture of uncertainty, according to many of those most actively involved in the ceasefire process, this would be to miss the underlying point. Not only are many of the main protagonists and battlefield foes now in dialogue (and experience from Northern Ireland to Palestine or South Africa has demonstrated how long it can take to lead from ceasefires to reform), but many long war-torn regions are also at their first peace in decades. This, in itself, is seen as an enormous first step. Foreign tourists now travel the road through Lashio, whereas only four years ago the most usual sights were army convoys or business trucks heading backwards and forwards pursuing China trade.

Certainly, no one is expecting the next stages to be easy. Given Burma's troubled past, failure can never be ruled out, and, indeed, a new generation of difficulties is only just beginning. Nevertheless, there remains a belief that if Burma's deep political problems are ever to be resolved, the establishment of peace is a priority, and this must eventually spread to those areas where fighting is still continuing so that the vexed issues of ethnic minority rights are addressed in tandem with democracy and greater national reform.[22]

So, as the ceasefire movement edges towards its first decade, questions will inevitably arise over what has actually been achieved in the field. This is an especially important question for international NGOs who are now working or considering working within Burma's complex parameters. Socially and politically, there can be no doubt over need—only over the feasibility of implementation.

The short answer, of course, is that all sides in the ceasefires have agreed to place immediate political problems to one side, including questions of state, while different initiatives are begun (such as health, business, and education) to try and cement the peace by finding new methods and institutions for effective social representation and progress. This may appear an uncertain scenario for international agencies, who have to decide whether, how, and with whom they should engage, but this is the reality that they must confront in whatever part of Burma they become engaged.

There may also be a temptation for the international community to try and create different models or agendas, but as Mark Duffield and

John Ryle have warned, in the final analysis effective actions can only be based upon real understanding of the peoples, realities, and problems of state as they exist on the ground. Thus in Burma's case, although the term "civil society" itself is not much discussed, it is important to recognize that there are different protagonists and peoples in Burma who are now urgently trying, in their own ways, to build confidence and strengthen elements in their own societies with the view to reform. This is a struggle as vital for the future peace and stability of Burma as the more-publicized questions of political deadlock and drama in Rangoon. As Nai Shwe Kyin, the eighty-four-year-old president of the New Mon State Party, told a press conference in October 1996 after forty-five years in the "underground" as an insurgent leader:

> We want to establish peace in our country. It is not a time to confront each other because we need national reconciliation. We have reached cease-fire agreements and the next step is political dialogue. We must establish trust. After bloodbaths lasting nearly half a century, we must establish trust with the view that one day reconciliation will come about.[23]

BURMA'S "OPEN DOOR": ASPECTS OF LIFE IN MINORITY REGIONS TODAY

Generalizing on particulars of life in ethnic minority regions of Burma today is a very fraught task. As described above, depending on who is talking or which issue or region is being discussed, selective evidence can be used to demonstrate both successes or failures in recent history—as well as to add fuel to the "politics or development" debate over which processes will bring lasting reform. The possible political dimensions, therefore, are many, but they are not the subject of this paper, which, instead will attempt to describe aspects of life in ethnic minority regions, where there is now the potential—although not necessarily the right—for greater international access. In keeping with the analysis in this paper, a particular emphasis will also be given to developments from the ethnic minority perspective, which, after all, is ultimately the key to the durability of peace and lasting reform.

For the uninitiated, traveling around ethnic minority regions of

Burma today can be a very puzzling experience. A decade ago, most such regions were officially off-limits from the Rangoon side, but in the former war zones visitors today will see, in addition to government troops, ethnic forces with a variety of different uniforms or insignia as well as trucks and new businesses bearing many new logos. Such complexities are also reflected in the bureaucracies of government as well as in the many different civilian groups. Indeed, negotiating between the different organizations—or even ascertaining what may or may not be possible—is never straightforward.

Not all ethnic minority areas, of course, are war zones, although many of the same basic difficulties prevail. But in the ceasefire areas, at least, the first practicality to be taken on board is that virtually all the ceasefire agreements have their own differences, and this often has as much to do with the relative strengths and weaknesses of the different military forces in the region (including the Burmese armed forces) as with the character or goals of the different protagonists. The KIO and UWSP, for example, control substantial standing armies as well as large regions of territory, while the NMSP and KNPP, by the time of their 1995 ceasefire agreements, had largely been pinned back to the Thai border where their troops were demarcated scattered "flag" positions out of which permission is needed to move. (Government forces similarly need permission to enter or cross armed opposition territory.)

However such limitations are not, in themselves, a major stumbling block. Indeed, from the perspective of civil society, the ceasefire forces should only be considered one element in the much more complicated social mosaic. This has long been understood by leaders on all sides, especially ethnic minority groups who have already begun to shy away from such terms as "war zones" or "ceasefire territories," preferring, instead, the much broader term "war-affected" to describe the broader communities of their peoples. Although long in use, armed struggle is a tactic, not a goal, of most nationalist movements, and it has always been a major source of grief and political concern that many minority communities have become divided way beyond the current frontlines of conflict.

Thus, regardless of strength, one of the first and most notable impacts of the ceasefires has been the ability of long-separated communities to openly reestablish contacts and for representatives of formally opposing groups to have access (although conditional) to formally restricted areas in each other's territory. This includes towns, villages, seacoasts, and borderlands as well as the many natural resources they contain. This, in turn, raises difficult questions over "give and take," but, in the search for peace, all sides initially decided that this was a gamble that had to be taken. In effect, a high-risk strategy had been embarked upon which a number of key opponents privately recognize could be far more dangerous to their individual interests than actually continuing the war.

From these initial steps towards peace, then, subsequent developments in "war-affected" areas can be divided into two main categories: the political and the social, both of which have implications for civil society. It is still very early days yet, but, given their marginalization in the past, many ethnic minority leaders believe that a number of significant points have already been established for the future.

From this perspective, the first important breakthrough has been that of political recognition, even if tangible or constitutional agreements have yet to be made. Fueling this desire for respect in the governmental arena has been a long-held belief that ethnic minority communities have often paid the highest price for the general political volatility in the country at large, and this, they claim, has happened on at least four occasions in the recent past: 1948, 1958–60, post-1962, and 1988.[24]

This time, during what all sides recognize may well be a rare moment of political reorientation, they want, like the *Tatmadaw* or NLD, to be on the inside of the political process in Rangoon. Certainly, few are prepared to trust their fate to Burman-majority parties. "For the KIO, the most important thing is that we become a legal party during this period of constitutional change," the late KIO chairman Brang Seng told this writer. "We have already lived through three different periods of government since 1961, so we know what it is like to be forgotten. For over thirty years, we have been described as terrorists and opium smugglers, and we have never been recognized."[25] In any transitional process, then, the legal acceptance of nationalist movements who genuinely represent the aspirations of their people is a key step in the establishment of civil society, and they are now theoretically able to legally act.

For the present, it should be stressed that any reform or transitional process is uncertain. The SLORC/SPDC's chosen vehicle for constitutional discussion, the National Convention, rarely met during 1996–97, and not only the NLD but also many ethnic minority parties have not been attending. In addition, new "self-administered" zones have been promised for the Wa, Pao, Palaung, Danu, Kokang, and Naga, but specific details have not been discussed on most ethnic minority issues. Instead, most attention has focused on the self-proclaimed "leading role in national political life" that the military government has been seeking to preserve for the *Tatmadaw*.[26] Uncertainties also remain over how ethnic minority forces that are still fighting—notably Karen and Shan who make up the country's largest ethnic minority populations—will eventually be brought, like the NLD, into the same reform discussions.

Nevertheless, in many ethnic minority regions of the country, there is undoubtedly a greater freedom of association and mobility within society than in recent decades. On a political level, for example, previously divided Kachin factions have now achieved a consensus, while the armed opposition PNO and the Union Pao National Organization, which won seats in the 1990 election, run themselves in tandem. Similar exchanges have taken place between different Shan parties and organizations, while in northeast Burma four of the ceasefire armies have formed a Peace and Democratic Front to try and broaden cooperation.

Most of these organizations also run schools, hospitals and their own local administrations, and they also interact with other community groups, including business companies and religious organizations. In addition, they also liaise, often closely, with different levels of the government, from both local *Tatmadaw* outposts to different ministries in Rangoon.

However, although elsewhere in the world international NGOs have often become involved in such "crisis" situations through running local training courses in "political" topics (such as democratization, conflict resolution, institution building, and media training), this is not generally regarded a realistic option at present in the field in ethnic minority regions of Burma. For the moment, the first emphasis is usually on humanitarian and development issues, and, in most respects, the military government still prefers to deal with inter-governmental organizations, especially the UN. If any reminder were needed, the extraordinary withdrawal of the International Committee of the Red Cross (ICRC) from Burma in June 1995 (over lack of standard ICRC access to prisoners) demonstrated just how difficult the operating context for international NGOs can be.

This, then, leads to the second arena of recent developments: the social. An important element here is economic, which is not dealt with in detail in this paper. For the moment, with the exception of the Total/Unocal pipeline and cross-border logging, international commercial (or development) organizations have penetrated relatively little into ethnic minority regions. But suffice to say, economic regeneration is one of the foremost aims of ethnic minority organizations and leaders. Compared to the restrictions of the past, there has been a relative upsurge in business activities, although, as elsewhere in Burma, serious problems remain and many communities are still living at subsistence level. Indeed, a number of ceasefire forces have, to date, been depending largely on revenues from logging, precious stones, and other natural resources, as well as the opium trade which still continues to thrive in parts of the Shan state.

However, as evidence of deeper change, ceasefire organizations such as the New Democratic Army on the China border have developed their own hydroelectric plants, while the KIO has reopened the large sugar mill at Namti, and the NMSP and SSA have both invested in fishing fleets on the Andaman Sea. Parallel to these developments, many local entrepreneurs have set up a host of new companies of their own, although it remains very much to be seen whether the people, in general, become "stakeholders" in the newly emerging economies in these regions. Without capital or development assistance, many communities have already complained that they find it difficult to compete.

Thus it is in the aid and humanitarian areas of social reform that most local or grassroots energies have been directed—and it is in this capacity that international agencies have become involved. This has been through both actual presence in the field, including both UN agencies and international NGOs, as well as through funding which has been channeled through local organizations in the community. It is also very striking that, ever since Medecins Sans Frontieres (Netherlands) and World Vision (UK) pioneered the return of NGOs to Burma after 1991, virtually all the agencies that have subsequently followed have mostly operated in the health field.[27] The same pattern is now also emerging in ethnic minority areas.

A pencil sketch of health and humanitarian problems certainly confirms the extent of need:[28]

- Decades of constant warfare have devastated many communities; even government leaders have confirmed over one million deaths in the fighting since 1948.[29]
- Only one third of the country has access to clean water and proper sanitation, little of which is available in minority areas.
- Burma has one of the highest rates of maternal and infant mortality in Asia, rates which are again probably highest in minority areas. For example, in contrast to the already high "national" Infant Mortality Rate (IMR), which has been variously estimated at between 47 and 94 deaths per 1,000 live births in the last few years, doctors in Karen and Shan state war zones have calculated IMR figures as high as 200 to 300 per 1,000 live births.
- With only one doctor for every 12,500 people, national health care does not even extend to half the area covered by the country's 319 townships, and again, notably, not to ethnic minority areas.
- Since 1988, Burma has become the world's largest producer of illicit opium and heroin, much of it produced in the Shan state, with an annual opium harvest of over two thousand tons. Again, the scourge of drug addiction and the attendant social problems are especially felt in minority communities.
- HIV/AIDS is increasing at alarming rates, with national estimates of HIV-carriers increasing from near zero to 500,000 over the past seven years. Again, such local problems as intravenous drug use, the migration of sex-workers and other transient laborers are particular factors in the disturbing scale of these problems in many minority communities.
- Burma has generated over one million refugees or internally displaced peoples as a result of the long civil wars.
- Finally, it is treatable or preventable illnesses, such as pneumonia, tuberculosis, malnutrition, diarrhea, and malaria, which are the largest causes of unnecessary death and suffering in Burma. Again, though problematic throughout the country,

it is often in ethnic minority regions that these problems are most acute. Few international health teams, however, have penetrated the hills to witness the conditions first hand.[30]

Briefly, then, in recent years a new start has been made in many minority communities to try to confront such serious health issues. For aid and development agencies there remain very real problems over accurate information and access to all parts of the country, while in too many areas the underlying causes of suffering, such as armed conflict, forced labor, or village relocations, remain unaddressed.

Nevertheless, in the ceasefire areas, the greater freedom and safety in travel has meant better access for many communities to the facilities in the towns (mostly private and expensive), while new clinics under the government's BADP have reportedly brought health outreach into new areas, although shortages of medicine are, as elsewhere in Burma, a perennial problem.

In another change since 1988, the government-backed NGOs (or GONGOs), the Myanmar Medical Association (MMA), Myanmar Red Cross (MRC), and Myanmar Maternal and Child Welfare Association (MMCWA) have also become more active, but again many of their programs are town-based, where they work in conjunction with the local Township Medical Officers who, in turn, come under the Ministry of Health. The quasi-political Union Solidarity and Development Association is also being increasingly mobilized for such local health programs.

Meanwhile, many of the ceasefire organizations, as well as religious-based groups (including Buddhists, Christians, and Muslims) have begun to launch programs of their own. Many of these programs, especially emergency relief, continued during the fighting, but since the ceasefires, much greater emphasis has been given to resettlement, as well as health, skills training, and education. In none of these areas has there been a set program or plan, but different organizations have generally used what resources and means they have at their disposal.

Since the ceasefire, for example, the KIO has resettled, under its own auspices, around 10,000 refugees from China and, with the aid of international NGOs, has been able to institute the first immunization program for children in the hills in recent history. Looking to the future, the KIO has also begun an extensive reforestation program and in 1997, for the first time ever, KIO and government military units began a joint opium eradication scheme, destroying over eight hundred acres of planted poppies. At the same time, in rather more difficult circumstances, the NMSP in southeast Burma has attempted to resettle—also with aid from international NGOs—over 8,000 refugees from Thailand, although here economic difficulties, continuing tensions and the 1997 floods have brought little respite to the sufferings of the Mon people.

Meanwhile, in the towns and rural villages, Christian church groups, in particular, from a number of different denominations, have become increasingly active in both relief work as well as education and training. In addition to power generation, sanitation, and well-building, job skills in such cottage industries as carpentry and tailoring are regarded as especially important to try and help anchor dislocated communities back in their homes. In response to another urgent need, HIV/AIDS awareness training has accelerated and, with help from different international NGOs (financial as well as training), many at-risk communities and sectors of society have now been targeted and reached.

In Christian communities especially, the understanding and coordination with international NGOs has often been easier to establish. Firstly, as a result of past travel and pastoral study trips abroad, many church workers and leaders in Burma are familiar with the care and development contexts of many Christian organizations in the modern world. Secondly, the very organization of local congregations—with women's groups, youth groups, children's groups, etc.—makes it much easier to implement different community projects. Indeed, long before Burma's "open door," many pastors and church organizations had established their own local projects (e.g. kindergartens), where a need was perceived in the community.

By contrast, the involvement of Buddhist groups in this deeply religious land has been more limited. Partly, this is due to the greater political problems in the country at large, where a number of monks and monasteries have been involved in anti-government protests since 1988; thus, the organization and practice of the Buddhist *sangha* remains a sensitive issue. But partly, too, there is no tradition for Buddhist monks in Burma to become involved in the same array of NGO and development projects as today exists in, for example, neighboring Thailand. Nevertheless, Buddhist monks do play a pivotal role in many communities, and the general scope of their activities can be expected to increase in future years.

In minority regions, for example, monks from the government-backed "Mountain Mission" have monasteries in all seven ethnic minority states, where, like many Christian churches, they have established dormitories so that orphans and children from the war zones or remote hills can come to study in the towns. Equally important, although details are still unclear, in the past few years government spokespersons have several times urged that the monasteries should (or can) run local primary schools, a role they once widely performed in the past and have continued in many rural villages until the present.

It is, therefore, into this still evolving array of new contexts that international NGOs must fit. Initially, as mentioned above, it appeared that the government preferred only to allow access to UN agencies. Since 1991, for example, the UNDP and UNDCP have begun pilot crop-substitution programs in the Shan state, UNICEF and WHO have both instituted various health and HIV/AIDS awareness projects in a number of targeted regions, while the UNHCR has become involved in the resettlement of the 250,000 Muslim refugees that were returning from Bangladesh.[31]

Nevertheless, in October 1994, in apparent line with the opening of the door to NGOs elsewhere in the country, a decision was made by the SLORC to accept "offers" of assistance from international agencies and NGOs in areas covered by the Border Areas Development Program, "as long as they do not threaten national security and solidarity."[32] To date, the majority of foreign NGOs that have established a permanent presence in Burma remain largely Rangoon-based, but in the past four years visits by foreign aid workers to once forbidden towns such as Myitkyina, Lashio, or Loikaw have become almost commonplace. Some have returned to establish programs (HIV/AIDS education is again a common theme), while others have funded programs through local community groups on the ground. There is, as yet, no common structure, system, or method to be found. Rather, as elsewhere in the world where humanitarian needs are regarded as urgent, the first priority is very often to get aid through to the people—and the practicalities are left to be sorted out later.

Finally, just as the evolution of engagement has been described, it is necessary to highlight—from the perspective of civil society—some of the more pertinent problems or obstacles as they have occurred. This can only be a brief summary, but a number of difficult issues have already emerged.

The first is undoubtedly a shortage of trained personnel to implement many aid and development schemes on the ground. In ethnic minority regions, decades of warfare have decimated many communities, disrupting all educational progress. As a result, many organizations and communities in the field are still headed by aging or inexperienced individuals who, although well-motivated, often do not have the vision or skills for the immense tasks ahead. Education must be revived.

A second major problem is the dearth of accurate information, and most especially information which reflects the divisions in society. Malaria and HIV/AIDS are often picked out as urgent or "fashionable" health issues, but cholera epidemics still pass unreported in the hills, while tuberculosis and various water-borne diseases also take a constant toll in human life. Epidemiologists already point out the inherent failures in tackling any such health issues with only access to partial information or from only one side of the community.

This, then, leads to a third major difficulty for international NGOs: what organizations or institutions they should work with or through. As discussed above, at a time of political volatility and transition, there are already many institutions and organizations in the field, including government departments, government-backed NGOs such as the MMCWA or USDA, opposition groups such as the NLD, ceasefire organizations and their various departments, church and Buddhist groups, and, finally, headmen and the local village structures themselves. Clearly, the choices are not obvious, if priority is given to the notion of civil society, which may be arbitrary, rather than to humanitarian need, where lives can be saved. Moreover, although there are now a few beginnings, truly independent or single-issue NGOs have yet to become numerous or firmly established in Burma away from the patronage or umbrella of the above structures and institutions.

Initially, a number of UN agencies, in line with the requirement of the UNDP's Governing Council to work at the grassroots level, chose to work through the government and its preferred NGOs or GONGOS. UNICEF, for example, helped develop a national project on the "Control of HIV/AIDS through Reproductive Health" in conjunction with the Ministry of Health and the ministry's three chosen NGOs, the MRC, MMCWA, and MMA. Generally, such programs have been regarded as successful and also valuable training in different health practices for Burmese health workers and institutions.

A similar approach was also taken by the UNHCR in the resettlement of Muslim refugees from Bangladesh. Significantly, too, in addition to the MRC and MMCWA, the French NGO, Action Internationale Contre la Faim, was brought in to support their work. However, while enhancing the profile of both domestic and international NGOs, criticisms quickly emerged in such minority regions over the UNHCR's choice of its Burmese implementing agencies, especially after refugees complained of the lack of trained medical staff who could speak their language, understand their customs, or were sensitive to the cultures of Muslim women.

More recently, concerns have been expressed elsewhere over the extent to which the MMCWA, MRC, and USDA are dominated by the government. It has been reported, for example, that throughout the country the wives of the local government (LORC/PDC) chairmen are also expected to act as chairpersons of the local MMCWA (although, at the local level, it should be mentioned that health workers do not necessarily see this as a problem). It is still also by no means clear where the real decision making and divisions of power lie between different government departments, such as the Ministry of Health, Border Areas Development Program, and Ministry of Social Welfare. That there are many committed officials in all these organizations and departments is not in doubt, but individual support and personal patronage still count for much. Moreover, in the field, local military commanders frequently have the last say.

It was in response to such concerns that Aung San Suu Kyi wrote to Mr. Gustave Speth, administrator of the UNDP, in January 1996, complaining of the discrimination that many citizens felt in gaining access to aid and requesting that, in future, UN agencies should consider ways of implementing programs "in close co-operation with the NLD;" in this way, Daw Suu Kyi argued, the UN would be working with the only organization in Burma which, through the 1990 election result, had been shown to represent the "will of the people."[33] To such comments, the military government's response was immediately hostile.

However, international NGOs which try to avoid the above dilemmas by turning to other community groups will find other problems waiting in store. For example, to date, the government has accepted the pastoral and humanitarian work undertaken by various church-based groups, as long as it is carried out under "evangelical" auspices. Indeed, many *Tatmadaw* leaders have been openly supportive and praised the work of such groups. However, despite the recent encouragement of Buddhist monastery schools, a similar degree of social work is not allowed— and, indeed, may be deliberately discouraged—amongst Buddhist groups. At the same time, it should be stressed that many Christian and Buddhist organizations want to continue as they are; not only are there issues of institutional capacity but many religious leaders would oppose any socio-political agendas outside their spiritual-holy remit or which they felt were, in other ways, unsuitable.

Similarly, although many international NGOs have long had cross-border contact with various armed ethnic opposition organizations, some are clearly better supported by their people and more able than others. Since the ceasefires, for example, some organizations have recognized that they have to evolve politically, socially, economically, and militarily—especially if they are to build social bridges within the community; they thus cannot afford to stand still. There are other forces, however, where individual leaders and military commanders have built up personal fortunes by monopolizing on trade (including, in some cases, opium), leading the Shan academic, Chao Tzang Yawnghwe, to claim that the ceasefire movement represents a new cultural evolution in Burmese politics: a new informal alliance between "warlords" in the "Burman" and "government" spheres (governmental warlords) and those in the "non-Burman" and "non-governmental" spheres (non-governmental warlords).[34]

This, then, finally leads to what, in the short term, may be the greatest difficulty for international NGOs in instituting effective programs in the ethnic minority regions of Burma. If aid is given to only one sector, faction, or group within such culturally diverse communities, not only can this be politically, socially, or religiously divisive, it could actually fuel even deeper grievances and misunderstandings. This has already been privately acknowledged within many ethnic minority communities, and, in the long term, it is felt that such problems can be confronted and dealt with. In the meantime, however, insensitive actions by international NGOs could precipitate and not heal the divisions.

As one Burmese physician told this writer:

> All this talk about communities and NGOs has become a bit of a smokescreen which every side can use. If health standards are really to improve, what is really needed is an integrated approach, where every health agency is energized and health information and techniques are freely shared and acted upon. This is simply not happening at present. Burma is still very socially divided.

In a nutshell, then, this is the dilemma which faces international NGOs concerning every area of development and engagement in Burma. Real reform and the establishment of civil society requires that every sector of society is empowered and involved. In essence, this means that state institutions, which are currently weak and underperforming, must be engaged as much as political parties, indigenous NGOs, and any institutions of democratic society. There is no country in the world where such varied issues as HIV/AIDS, education, or political and economic policy would be dealt with in any other way.

So, in conclusion, recent history in Burma including the pro-democracy movement and the ceasefire process, has at last brought many protagonists together or, at least, concentrated minds to think seriously about the future. Hope is alive, but there is still a very long way to go. In the meantime, international NGOs may well find that if they are realistic and sensitive to the needs of the people, they can work at the local level, but it is also vital that they should never lose sight of the bigger picture.

APPENDIX: STATUS OF ARMED ETHNIC OPPOSITION GROUPS, JULY 1998

Main Ceasefire Organizations (in order of agreement)	Leader	Year
Myanmar National Democratic Alliance Army (Kokang)	Pheung Kya-shin	1989
United Wa State Party (or Myanmar National Solidarity Party)	Pauk Yo Chang	"
National Democratic Alliance Army (eastern Shan state)	Lin Ming Xian	"
Shan State Army/Shan State Progress Party*	Sai Nawng	"
New Democratic Army (in northeast Kachin state)	Ting Ying	"
Kachin Defense Army (KIO 4th Brigade)	Mahtu Naw	1991
Pao National Organization*	Aung Kham Hti	"
Palaung State Liberation Party*	Aik Mone	"
Kayan National Guard (breakaway group from KNLP)	Htay Ko	1992
Kachin Independence Organization*	Zau Mai	1994
Karenni State Nationalities Liberation Front	Tun Kyaw	"
Kayan New Land Party*	Shwe Aye	"
Shan State Nationalities Liberation Organization	Tha Kalei	"
New Mon State Party*	Nai Shwe Kyin	1995

Other Ceasefire Forces (not always announced or listed by government)		
Democratic Karen Buddhist Army	U Thuzana	1995
Mongko Region Defense Army (splinter group from Kokang)	Mong Hsala	"
Shan State National Army (frontline status often unclear)	Gun Yawd	"
Mong Tai Army	Khun Sa	1996
Karenni National Defense Army (splinter faction from KNPP)	Lee Rey	"
Karen Peace Force (ex-KNU 16th Battalion)	Tha Mu Hei	1997
Communist Party of Burma (Arakan province)	Saw Tun Oo	"
Mergui Mon Army (splinter faction from NMSP)	Ong Suik Heang	"

Non Ceasefire Forces**		
Arakan Liberation Party*	Khine Ye Khine	
Chin National Front*	Thomas Thangnou	
Karen National Union* (1995–6 talks broke down)	Bo Mya	
Karenni National Progressive Party* (1995 ceasefire broke down)	Hte Buphe	
Lahu National Organization*	Paya Ja Oo	
Mergui-Tavoy United Front (ex-CPB, mainly Tavoyans)	Saw Han	
Mon Army Mergui District (splinter faction from NMSP)	Nai Sein Hla	
National Socialist Council of Nagaland		
{NSCN (East)	Khaplang	
{NSCN (Main faction)	Muivah	
National Unity Party of Arakan (ex-National Unity Front of Arakan)	Shwe Tha	
Rohingya National Alliance		
{Arakan Rohingya Islamic Front	Nurul Islam	
{Rohingya Solidarity Organization	Dr. Yunus	
Shan United Revolutionary Army (reformed 1996 after MTA surrender)	Yord Serk	
Wa National Organization* (1997 talks broke down)	Maha San	

Source: Smith, *Burma* (1998 ed.), chart 3.

* Former or current National Democratic Front member

** A handful of other small, armed groups also exist in name. Most are affiliated to the Democratic Alliance of Burma. Only the Burman majority All Burma Students Democratic Front has any real organization inside Burma.

NOTES

1. These issues are analyzed more fully in, Martin Smith, *Burma: Insurgency and the Politics of Ethnicity* (London and New Jersey: Zed Books, 1991 [new edition 1998]) pp. 322–401.

2. See e.g., Andrew Selth, *Burma's Defence Expenditure and Arms Industries* (Working Paper No. 309, Australian National University, Strategic and Defence Studies Center, August 1997).

3. The 702 delegates to the National Convention, which was first convened in January 1993, included representatives of eight categories: elected MPs, representatives of other legal parties, ethnic nationalities, peasants, workers, civil servants, intellectuals and other specially invited guests. Since 1988, the military government has always distinguished between "national politics," which it sees—like national security and national unity—as its exclusive preserve, and "party politics," which, it says, are the responsibility of democratic organizations and parties.

4. David Steinberg, *Burma: Prospects for Political and Economic Reconstruction* (World Peace Foundation and Harvard Institute for International Development, WPF Reports No. 15, 1997) p. 39.

5 . The Kachin Independence Organization reaffirmed in a press release on 16 April 1997: "At this critical moment, the KIO thus trusts that all parties will reflect on the tragic lessons of Burma's recent history, confirm a new commitment to the establishment of trust and national understanding, and find ways to support peace and dialogue as the immediate bridges to heal the divisions of the past."

6. See e.g., *Kyemon*, 4 July 1996, *New Light of Myanmar*, 4 October 1996.

7 . Total, Unocal, PTTEP, MOGE, *The Yadana Gas Development Project* (Paris, 1997), pp. 6–7; for a contrasting view, see, KNU Mergui/Tavoy District, *Development and the Cry of the People* (Mergui/Tavoy, 1994), and, Earthrights International and Southeast Asian Network, *Total Denial* (Kanchanaburi, 1996).

8. Mark Duffield, *Evaluating Conflict Resolution: Context, Models and Methodology* (Discussion paper prepared for the Chr. Michelsen Institute, Bergen, Norway, May 1997) p. 6.

9. See e.g., UNDP, *Summary Report: UNDP Assistance to Myanmar (as per GC decision 93/ 21)* (Rangoon, May 1995); Agrodev Canada Inc, *UNDP's Human Development Initiative: An Assessment* (Ontario, January 1995).

10. John Ryle, October 1997 Nuffield Lecture (Oxford), as extracted in *Guardian* (London) 22 November 1997.

11. *Bangkok Post*, 22 November 1997.

12. For an analysis of this issue from the SLORC's perspective, see, Aung Min, "Can there be a Kachin republic?," *Working People's Daily*, 14 March 1993.

13. Barry Buzan, *People, States, and Fear: The National Security Problem in International Relations* (Brighton: Wheatsheaf Books, 1983) pp. 66–7.

14. See e.g., Smith, *Burma*, pp. 89, 400.

15. For example, there were hundreds of fatalities of both villagers and combatants during September–October 1988 in nonstop battles after the CPB briefly captured the town of Mong Yang in eastern Shan state and the KNU overran Mae Tah Waw adjoining the Thai border. Then in December, 106 government troops were killed and 15 captured in a single ambush by a joint CPB-KIO force near Kongsa, Kutkai district, in the northern Shan state.

16. Shortly after their mutiny, the UWSP made a broadcast on the former CPB radio station aimed at troops on the government side: "Every year the burden on the people has become heavier. The streams, creeks and rivers have dried up, while the forests are being depleted. At such a time, what can the people of all nationalities do?"; see, Smith, *Burma*, p. 423.

17. For a brief discussion of a program which has been treated with skepticism by government critics, see, Martin Smith, *Ethnic Groups in Burma: Development, Democracy and Human Rights*

(London: Anti-Slavery International, 1994) pp. 100–2. Subsequently, the BADP claimed 228 million kyats (or US$ 38 million) was spent in the first two years on such projects as road-building, health care and schools, with 727 million kyats (or US$ 121 million) projected for the next six years. See also, e.g., BADP, *Measures Taken for Development of Border Areas and National Races (3)* (Rangoon, 1992), which includes descriptions of many minority areas, both ceasefire and non-ceasefire; and, Lt-Col. Thein Han, "Unity in Diversity," in Office of Strategic Sudies, *Human Resource Development and Nation Building in Myanmar* (Ministry of Defense, Rangoon, 1997) pp. 215–230.

18. See e.g., US Department of State, *Plan for Implementation of Section 570 of Conference Report 104-863 to Accompany H.R. 3610* (Omnibus Appropriations Act, 1997), submitted to US Congress 13 June 1997. Notably, US policy towards Burma today seeks progress in three key areas: democracy, human rights and counter-narcotics.

19. See also, n.3. The National Convention, which is still intermittently continuing, is beyond the theme of this paper. Eventually, like the NLD, a number of ethnic minority parties have either been banned or cease to attend. Similarly, representatives of some ceasefire groups (e.g. PNO, UWSP) have attended, while others have either not been invited or have stayed away. Nevertheless, from the perspective of institutions, it should be noted that, as of mid-1995, delegates of eight ethnic minority parties which had legally stood in the 1990 election, were still attending: Shan Nationalities League for Democracy, United Karen League, Union Pao National Organization, Shan State Kokang Democratic Party, Mro (or Khami) Unity Organization, Kokang Democracy and Unity Party, Lahu National Development Party, and Wa National Development Party. Indeed, representatives of only two other "legal" parties, the pro-government National Unity Party (ex-BSPP) and the NLD, which has since withdrawn, were also still in attendance. For a discussion, see, Janelle M. Diller, "The National Convention: An Impediment to the Restoration of Democracy," in, Peter Carey (ed.), *Burma: The Challenge of Change in a Divided Society* (Basingstoke and New York: Macmillan Press and St. Martin's Press, 1997) pp. 27–54.

20. See e.g., Smith, *Burma*, pp. 333–5, 339–44.

21. Note by the Secretary General, *Situation of Human Rights in Myanmar* (Fifty-second session, Agenda Item 112 (c), 6 October 1997) paras. 75–6.

22. Only the KNU, SURA, and, to a lesser extent, KNPP remain opposition forces of any real size without ceasefires at the time of writing. However, small Chin, Naga, Rakhine and "Rohingya" Muslim forces (see appendix) also still operate along the India and Bangladesh borders where they act as a reminder of the historic scale of ethnic discontent within the country.

23. *Reuters*, 2 October 1996.

24. I.e., post-independence in 1948, during Ne Win's Caretaker Administration of 1958–60, after General Ne Win seized power in the 1962 (when many of the government's Burman opponents, including both the CPB and the deposed prime minister U Nu, waged armed struggle from ethnic minority lands), and, finally, after the pro-democracy uprising in 1988.

25 . See, Martin Smith, "Burma at the Crossroads," *Burma Debate*, November/December 1996, p. 12.

26. It has already been announced, for example, that 25 percent of all seats in the future parliament must be reserved for military candidates. See also, n.3 and n.19.

27. By 1995, for example, at least fifteen NGOs had representatives or programs in the country. Not all had Memoranda of Understanding and some later left or were rejected by the SLORC, but amongst other NGOs reported to be present were: Action Internationale Contre la Faim, Adventist Development and Relief Agency, Association Francois-Xavier Bagnoud, Australian Red Cross, Bridge Asia Japan, Care International, Groupe de Recherche et d'Echanges Technologiques, International Committee of the Red Cross, International Federation of Eye

Banks, International Federation of the Red Cross and Red Crescent Societies, Leprosy Mission International, Medecins du Monde, Population Services International, Sasakawa Foundation, Save the Children (UK) and World Concern. Most only arrived in 1994–95.

28. The following statistics and health issues are analyzed more fully in Martin Smith, *Fatal Silence? Freedom of Expression and the Right to Health in Burma* (London: Article 19, 1996).

29. In 1989, in the first ever public admission of the scale of loss of life, the then SLORC chairman, Gen. Saw Maung, announced the true death toll in fighting since independence "would reach as high as millions, I think. It really is no good." He also revealed that 28,000 families in Burma were receiving pensions for soldiers that had been killed since 1953 and 40,000 for disabled veterans. On the armed opposition side, there is no exact data at all; for a discussion, see Smith, *Burma*, pp. 100–1.

30. See n.28 above.

31. See e.g., UNHCR, *Return to Myanmar: Repatriating Refugees from Bangladesh*, Information Bulletin, June 1995.

32. Smith, *Fatal Silence?*, p. 119.

33. Ibid.

34. Letter to the Editor, *Independence: The Shan Herald Agency for News*, Vol. 144, 20 July 1996, pp. 33–4. Other critics have suggested parallels to the discredited Ka Kwe Ye militia program of the 1960s and 70s, but government spokespersons are quick to reject this, arguing that this time all ceasefire forces are able to engage in "party politics."

NO ROOM TO MOVE: LEGAL CONSTRAINTS ON CIVIL SOCIETY IN BURMA

ZUNETTA LIDDELL

The development and maintenance of civil society—that is, free associations of citizens joined together to work for common concerns, or implement social, cultural, or political initiatives which compliment, as well as compete, with the state—depends upon the citizens of any state being able to enjoy fundamental freedoms: freedom of thought, opinion, expression, association, and movement. Underscoring and defending these freedoms must be an independent judiciary and the guarantee of the rule of law. In Burma today, none of these conditions exist.

There is no freedom of the press in Burma: government censorship is heavy-handed and pervasive. While the opening up of the economy since 1988 led to a proliferation of private magazines, and access to affordable video and satellite equipment resulted in a massive expansion of small scale video companies and TV/video parlors around the country, the organs of state censorship have kept pace with these developments, and virtually every sentence and every image which is produced by the indigenous media has to be passed by the government's censorship board. All non-local media are also carefully monitored and controlled. The Burmese services of the BBC, VOA, and the Oslo-based Democratic Voice of Burma are often jammed; CNN and World Service broadcasts which include issues sensitive to the government mysteriously lose sound. New laws have been promulgated to restrict access to the internet, and it has been reported that the government has purchased technology from Israel which can monitor and censor e-mail messages, as well as other equipment from Singapore to monitor satellite phones.[1]

Neither is there any freedom of association. There are no independent trade unions. Rather, civil servants, who form the vast majority of the professional, blue- and white-collar workers in the country, are forced, by a variety of coercive measures, into the government-backed Union Solidarity Development Association. Political parties were permitted to form for the first time in decades after the SLORC assumption of power in 1988, but of the over two hundred parties which registered then, only seven remained legal by 1993. More have since been formed by the ethnic minority groups which made ceasefire agreements with the SLORC between 1989 and 1993, but at the same time, some of those groups have still not been publicly removed from the list of unlawful associations under the 1975 Act of that name (more below). Significantly, among the first parties to be de-registered were those which represented ethnic minorities and which had collectively called for a federal constitution in their party manifestos.[2] Non-governmental organizations (NGOs) and professional associations in Burma must register with the government under the Companies Act, and thus far in this climate of fear and repression, few have. Those NGOs which do exist have either been coopted by the government at the highest levels, or were government-inspired NGOs in the first place.[3]

Since 1989 some fifteen armed ethnic opposition groups have formed ceasefire agreements with the government, though as yet the SLORC/SPDC has gone no further than this first step in what is hoped will be a process towards lasting political settlements. The ceasefires mark a major change in the climate in Burma, where previous military governments have appeared to consider military defeat as the only way to end the ethnic minority rebellions, This change may serve to create the conditions necessary for the development of civil society in areas which are at peace for the first time in decades. There is some dispute about the effects of the ceasefire agreements on the development of civil society in war-affected areas. However, at least in terms of legal considerations, they have not lead to the creation of a safe space where civil society–like structures can develop.

In sum, Burma is a highly authoritarian state, and the SLORC's administrative reforms since 1988 have all been aimed at greater centralization of economic and political power. This is perhaps hardly surprising given the role of professional groups, students unions, and *sangha* (Buddhist monks) organizations in the uprising of 1988 and in mass anti-government demonstrations since then. Resurrected trade unions organized a general strike which continued from mid-August through early October; the Rangoon Bar Council published a statement condemning the killing of civilians and saying that the armed forces were acting unconstitutionally and in violation of international law; the Burma Medical Association condemned the killings in Rangoon in August; and most importantly student unions and monks organizations were effectively in charge in several cities, including Mandalay, for nearly six weeks.[4] On taking power, the first thing the SLORC did was to outlaw strike centers and gatherings of five people or more on the streets.

There is no sign as yet that the newly created State Peace and Development Council (SPDC) will buck the centralizing trend. Indeed, within days of its creation, divisional, state, and township level Peace and Development Councils were formed, with a reportedly higher prevalence of military personnel than the previous Law and Order Restoration Councils. Given this situation, any moves towards civil society can only take place at the most local of local levels or for the most ephemeral events—in sections of the village, among church congregations or around Buddhist monasteries; or in township or even state level organizations for temple festivals, emergency relief work, national immunization campaigns and so on—where they cannot be perceived to be a threat to the state. Whether such local initiatives will ever be allowed to develop into national civil society–like structures is very doubtful. It is here that international NGOs have to be most careful: supporting local initiatives, especially if the support is financial as well as "technical," could result in them gaining the unwanted attention of officials in Rangoon who may then either coopt the group, or prevent them from operating.

I. THE LEGAL SYSTEM

Before any discussion of the laws themselves, it is important to note the lack of clarity and openness in Burma's legal system. On taking power in 1988 the SLORC "suspended" the 1974 constitution; thus there is no constitution currently in place to set legal limits on the actions of the SLORC/SPDC. Although without a constitution, the SLORC stated that all laws in place at the time of their taking power will remain in force unless otherwise stated in SLORC Declarations and Orders. Then, in July 1991 the SLORC formed a Law Scrutiny Central Board, chaired by the attorney-general, U Aung Toe. This board was charged with assessing all existing laws and appealing or amending those "found to be non-beneficial to the state and the people." I think it can be assumed that the main purpose of this body was to assess laws which contradicted or limited the development of a free market economy, and indeed many laws have since been appealed or new laws enacted which allow for the formation of joint venture companies, banking and other financial institutions, and so on. However, in March 1996 the SLORC told the UN Commission on Human Rights that this body had repealed 151 laws, though it did not give a list of those laws. In addition, after repeated demands from the International Labor Organization that the government repeal the 1908 Villages and Towns Acts which allows for the forced recruitment of labor, the SLORC stated in October 1997 that it had amended the two laws, but indicated that they would be included in the new constitution, rather than promulgated immediately.

Given this situation, and the fact that under the SLORC there has been no legal gazette, it is often very difficult to know which laws are in effect today.

Over and above these considerations, though, is the lack of an independent and impartial judiciary and due process of law. Between 1988 an 1992 all political prisoners were tried by military tribunals— summary courts often held within jails—at which the defendants had no right to legal representation or to call witnesses. Since the repeal of military tribunals in April 1992, things have not improved much for those arrested for their involvement in political parties or for violating laws limiting freedom of speech, association, and assembly. In addition, the rule of law in non-political cases is limited by gross corruption among the judiciary, the complete absence of any form of government-funded legal aid to the poor (which results in many cases being undefended), and the SLORC's appointment of judges who were former military officers with little experience of civil law. Burma's legal system under the SLORC has been repeatedly condemned by human rights organizations and the U.N. Special Rapporteur for not meeting international standards. Most recently, in his December 1997 report, the Special Rapporteur stated that

> the absence of an independent judiciary, coupled with a host of executive orders criminalizing far too many aspects of normal civilian conduct that prescribe enormously disproportionate penalties and authorize arrest and detention without judicial review or any other form of judicial authorization, leads the Special Rapporteur to conclude that a significant percentage of all arrests and detentions in Myanmar are arbitrary when measured against generally accepted international standards.

II. FREEDOM OF INFORMATION AND EXPRESSION

Perhaps the most notorious and certainly the most frequently used law limiting freedom of expression is the **1950 Emergency Provisions Act** (EPA). This act is very broadly worded and has been used against people who have done as little as sung pro-democracy songs or written letters to friends abroad which included critical remarks against the government. Section 5 states:

> He who . . . (e) causes or intends to spread false news knowing before hand it is untrue; . . . (j) causes or intends to disrupt the morality or the behavior of a group of people or the general public, or to disrupt the security or the reconstruction of the stability of the Union; . . . such a person shall be sentenced to seven years in prison, fine or both.

Scores of National League for Democracy members and supporters and other political dissidents have been sentenced under this act. Some of the best-known are:

- U Nay Min, arrested in 1988 for allegedly providing information to the BBC. He was sentenced to a total of fourteen years, which was reduced in the general amnesty in 1992 to ten years, and was finally released in November 1996, having been given the customary reduction of sentence for good behavior.
- Ye Htut, a student who was not politically active himself but

had friends among the ABSDF. He was sentenced in November 1995 to seven years under the EPA for having sent copies of the New Light of Myanmar and other periodicals in letters to his student friends abroad.

- Nine students arrested in April 1995 at the funeral of the former prime minister U Nu for having allegedly sung part of the song, "Kaba ma kyey bu," the pro-democracy anthem from 1988. They were each sentenced to seven years under the EPA.

In addition, the **Burma Penal Code, section 109**, allows for the arrest for up to seven years for people who "spread false information injurious to the state." The similarity of the wording between these two laws has meant that, following intense criticism from the Special Rapporteur and others over its use of the EPA, the SLORC has taken to using this section of the Penal Code to sentence NLD members and thus obscure the political nature of the alleged "crime." At other times, it has used both laws against the same person, for example, the author Daw San San Nwe who was sentenced to a total of ten years imprisonment in October 1994.

The **Printers and Publishers Registration Law (1962)** was brought in soon after the 1962 coup to limit and control what was at the time one of the most free and prolific media industries in Asia. The law established the Press Scrutiny Board which must censor all books, films, magazines and songs before publication. It also limits the numbers of copies which can be published. In June 1989 the law was amended to increase the punishments for non-compliance to imprisonment for up to ten years and fines of up to 30,000 kyats (currently about US $1,000, but officially US $5,000).

The **Official Secrets Act (1948)** allows for the detention of between three and ten years for anyone "handing over classified state documents of national interest to unauthorized persons," but has been used against people who have passed on documents not so classified and which could not reasonably be argued to be a threat to the national interest.

As if this were not enough to stifle opposition, last year the SLORC promulgated three laws aimed at preventing criticism of the national convention and curbing the use of new communications technology.

In June 1996 the SLORC promulgated a new law, SLORC **Order 5/96**, which essentially allowed for the detention for up to twenty years of anyone even verbally criticizing the National Convention, the government-run constitutional assembly, and also the banning of any party or organization which encourages its members to do so. The law reads:

> *. . . Law to protect the stable, peaceful and systematic transfer of state responsibility, and the successful implementation of the National Convention tasks from disruption and opposition. . . .*

Section 3. No person or organization is allowed directly or indirectly to violate either [sic] of the following prohibitions.

a. Instigating, protesting, preaching, saying (things) or writing and distributing materials to disrupt and deteriorate the stability of the state, community peace and tranquillity, and the prevalence of law and order.

b. Instigating, protesting, saying (things) or writing and distributing materials to affect and destroy the national consolidation.

c. Disrupting, destroying, hindering, instigating, preaching, saying (things) or writing and distributing materials to affect, destroy and belittle the tasks being implemented at the National Convention, which has been convened in order to draw up a firm constitution, and to cause misunderstanding among the people.

d. Implementing [sic] the tasks of the National Convention; or drawing up or writing and disturbing state constitution with no legal authorization.

e. Attempting or collaborating to violate any of the above mentioned prohibitions.

Section 4. Anyone who is convicted of violating the prohibitions mentioned in Section 3, shall be sentenced to a minimum of three years and a maximum of twenty years in jail and may be subjected to fines.

Section 5. If any organization or person violates the prohibitions mentioned in section 3 at the direct assistance from any organizations, that organization or organizations shall be:

a. Banned for a limited period,

b. Disbanded, or

c. Shall become an illegal organization.

In July, it was the **Television and Video Act** which required all UN agencies and foreign diplomatic missions to submit imported videos to be shown publicly to the scrutiny of the PSB. It also required all video-parlors to obtain licenses and that all videos be they locally produced or foreign, be approved by the video censorship board. Violations of this law carry three-year prison sentences and/or fines of up to 100,000 kyats.

The 27th of September saw the introduction of the **Computer Science Development Law** which made the unauthorized import, possession and use of computers with networking capacities, modems or any other means of transmitting information electronically, punishable with sentences of between seven and ten years.

> Section 34. Whoever commits any of the following acts using computer network or any information technology shall, on conviction, be punished with imprisonment for a term which may extend from a minimum of seven years to a maximum of ten years, and may also be liable to a fine.
>
> a. carrying out any act which undermines State Security, prevalence of law and order and community peace and tranquillity, national unity, state economy or national culture;
>
> b. obtaining or sending and distributing any information of State secret relevant to State security, prevalence of law and order and community peace and tranquillity, national unity, state economy or national culture . . .

Bizarrely, the law states that its objectives include "to contribute towards the emergence of a modern developed State through computer science."

While these laws have been used or are apparently directed mainly at political opponents, and specifically the NLD, they are so broadly worded that they enforce a great deal of self-censorship on all groups and individuals whose work could be interpreted as being critical of the government. In essence, in Burma, any critique of any government policy is taken by the government to be an attack on the government itself. The arrest last year of Win Htein and nine other NLD activists and farmers who were given lengthy jail terms for attempting to reveal the failures of the government's agricultural policy in the Irrawaddy delta region, has served to reinforce this self-censorship.

III. FREEDOM OF ASSOCIATION

The most far-reaching law prohibiting free association is SLORC **Order 2/88**, issued by then chairman of the SLORC, Gen. Saw Maung, on the day the SLORC assumed power, for all monks and people to abide by. It states:

a. No one, without proper authorization, is permitted to travel on the streets between 20.00 and 04.00.

b. Gathering, walking, marching in processions, chanting slogans, delivering speeches, agitating, and creating disturbances on the streets by a group of five or more people is banned regardless of whether the act is with the intention of creating disturbances or of committing a crime or not.

c. No one is permitted to open strike centers regardless of whether or not the intent is to cause disturbances or commit a crime.

d. No one is permitted to block roads or to demonstrate en masse.

e. No one is to interfere or to obstruct people carrying out security duties.

Section (a) of this Order was repealed in April 1992, when Gen. Than Shwe came to power, but the other sections remain in place. While this law has not often been enforced, there are many other laws which are. The most frequently used law is the 1908 (1957) **Unlawful Associations Act** which allows for the detention of up to three years of anyone who is a member of or assists in any way an unlawful association:

"Unlawful association" means an association—

a. which encourages or aids persons to commit acts of violence or intimidation or of which the members habitually commit such acts, or

b. which has been declared to be unlawful by the President of the Union under the powers hereby conferred.

17.1 Whoever is a member of an unlawful association or takes part in meetings of any such association or contributes or receives or solicits contributions for any such association, or in any way assists the operations of any such association, shall be punished with imprisonment for a term not less than two years or more than three years.

Other laws are aimed specifically at preventing civil servants, who, in a country where private institutions and businesses were effectively banned until 1988, make up the majority of the non-agricultural work force, from participating in politics. In 1990, the SLORC issued a law reiterating this, and further prohibiting their relatives from supporting political parties in any way. I quote the law in full because it has particular importance since the formation of the SPDC, and shows clearly how the government has in the first place broken all of its original promises in terms of opening up the political space for multi-party democracy, and in the second place, attempted to prevent any perceived or real alternative power structures from developing within its own ranks.

Order 1/90[5] was issued on 22 May 1990 to remind people that "action will be taken against all those who fail to report people illegally residing in their homes." Noting that under existing laws any person not normally resident in a house who stays for one night or more must be registered at the local township LORC office, it threatens to charge persons failing to do so under section 124 of the Criminal Code "for failing to disclose to the authorities concerned either an act or a conspiracy that amounts to high treason" and sentencing them to seven years' imprisonment, or three years' imprisonment under the Unlawful Association Act, section 17.1; or six months' imprisonment and a fine or both under section 22 of the Criminal Code for "failure to report the crimes committed." The order states that it was issued after the arrest of Myint Soe and Aung Naing, both members of the ABSDF, who were arrested in Rangoon having been found hiding there for some time. It states:

> 4. In order to peacefully and successfully hold the multi-party democratic elections on 27th May 1990 as well as to timely expose the destructive insurgents, it is vital to uncover insurgent sappers sent in by all sorts of insurgent organizations.

SLORC **Order 1/91**, promulgated on 30 April 1991, requires that the conduct of public service personnel be clear of party politics:

1. Since assuming the responsibilities of the state and in accordance with the wishes of the people, the SLORC has been undertaking the restructuring of the nation's political system. In doing so, the SLORC has been laying down the foundations for the transformation of the political system from a one-party system to a multi-party system by abolishing laws that protect the one-party system while promulgating other necessary laws. . . .

3a. public service personnel must not engage in any party politics. They must not provide financial assistance to or support by other means any political party.

b. They must not be a member of any political organization.

c. They must prohibit their dependents or persons under their guardianship from taking direct or indirect part in activities that are aimed at opposing the government.

d. They must not be party to any labor association, organization, union, and other like bodies not formed in accordance with the rules occasionally announced and prescribed by the government. . . .

IV. FREEDOM OF MOVEMENT

Freedom of movement—and the right to political participation—is controlled and restricted by the SLORC's control of the issuance of personal identity cards (ID cards). For decades, all residents in Burma have had to carry identity cards, showing the citizenship status, normal place of residence, date of birth, name of father, and so on. The format of these cards was changed in 1990 to include not only all of the above, but also ethnicity and religion. All residents and citizens in Burma were required to apply for the new cards, without which it is illegal to buy a train or bus ticket, to register with a local council outside one's normal place of residence, and to vote in any future elections (though, as with all things in Burma today, it is often possible if you can pay the required bribe). For many ethnic minorities, including those residing in territory formally held by insurgent armies or other war-affected areas, obtaining the new cards is extremely difficult, and for the Muslims Rohingyas of northern Arakan state, it is impossible.[6] Following ceasefire agreements with some ethnic groups, the government guaranteed all those residing in areas under the control of the ethnic group temporary ID cards which would be replaced with permanent cards once a formal check of their identities had been made. In the case of all former Mong Tai (Khun Sa) soldiers at least, this promise has not been fulfilled and the temporary cards have become worthless. In many other ethnic areas, many people have not been informed of the need to apply for the new cards, or have found that the processing procedures can be extremely lengthy. As a result, few ethnic minorities living outside of urban centers have ID cards, and thus, they have no right to vote.

In many war-affected areas—that is, regions where armed opposition groups either currently operate, have operated in, or occasionally pass through—freedom of movement and freedom to choose one's place of residence[7] are violated by forced relocations and forced evictions. In these areas these practices have been continuing for decades, and have been a major element of the Burmese armies' counter-insurgency policies. Most recently, since March 1995, the central Shan state and Karenni state have been particular targets of forced relocation/eviction programs intended to cut off all possible support to those rebel groups who have not yet signed ceasefire agreements. Over 300,000 people have been affected in the past two years, many of whom, if able to escape the relocation sites, have sought sanctuary in Thailand. In Burma's towns and cities the SLORC has paid scant regard to the civil rights of its citizens and embarked on a nationwide "cleanup" program of relocating the urban poor to new satellite towns, usually with minimal preparation for their welfare at the new sites.[8] The estimates of the total number of internally displaced in Burma range from 1 to 2 million people, though the true number will probably never be known.

The ability of Burmese citizens to move freely from Burma to other countries is also restricted by the government, which will only issue passports for limited periods (a maximum of two years). This system also enables the government to monitor and restrict the activities of those abroad, who have to go to the government embassy to renew their passports every two years. Failure to pay roughly 10 percent of all earnings while abroad (this tax is currently the government's main source of foreign exchange) or involvement in any political activities while abroad, results in a refusal to renew the passport, forcing the holder either to return to Burma or to seek political asylum.

V. THE BUDDHIST *SANGHA* (ORDER OF MONKS)

The examples above, which are in fact just a taste of the worst of Burma's laws which restrict or prohibit freedom of speech, assembly, and association, reveal just how tight state control is. Unsurprisingly, that control also extends to religious organizations, and in particular to the Buddhist *sangha*, which as a body has traditionally been at the forefront of social justice movements in Burma (e.g., 1930s independence movement, 1988 uprising). I mention the *sangha* here because it has been seen by some as a potential leader of civil society and a possible NGO partner. However, the *sangha*, while many of the over 300,000 monks and novices in Burma would like to be involved in social reform, as a body it is essentially a government-organized non-governmental organization (GONGO).

During the 1988 democracy period, the monks played a key role, especially in Mandalay, of keeping control and order during the demonstrations and at times negotiating with the military. In September 1990 monks in Mandalay and Rangoon demonstrated by refusing to accept alms or perform religious ceremonies for military families in order to try and force the government to recognize the results of the May election. This provoked a massive crackdown on the monks in which monasteries were raided and hundreds of monks arrested. In October the SLORC promulgated a new law banning all independent *sangha* organizations and limiting *sangha* sects to nine. Any monk convicted of violating the law by trying to form a new organization faced up to three years' imprisonment.

This law, while serious in itself, was in fact just another zipper to the government's straight-jacket control of the *sangha*. While the military since 1962 has been keen to present itself as a secular government, it maintained a close relationship with the *sangha*, both in order to increase its own legitimacy with the Burman population, and also, perhaps more importantly, to control "the purity" of the monks—and expel any monks who either express views opposing Buddhist doctrine, or government policy. In 1980 the *sangha* was purged, a purge conducted by the infamous butcher of Rangoon, Col. Sein Lwin, and it has been almost total. At that time, the government appointed a working committee of six monks which chose some one thousand monks to attend a *sangha* congregation in May 1980.[9] The congregation produced the "Fundamental Rules of Organization of the *Sangha*," the means by which the *sangha* ostensibly controlled and regulated itself, but since appointment to the relevant *sangha* committees is controlled by the Department of Religious Affairs, it was actually an extension of governmental control to "wayward" members of the *sangha*.[10] Hundreds of monks, including those practicing indigenous medicine, were thrown out of the *sangha* and their sects made illegal.

Buddhism and the state are inseparable in the SLORC's Burma, and a compliant *sangha* is essential to maintain its cloak of legitimacy. More than past regimes, the SLORC has an implicit "one nation, one race, one religion" ideology which is clear in all of its dealings with ethnic and religious minorities. For example, the August 1993 Development of Border Areas and National Races Law, includes in its objectives "to cherish and preserve the culture, literature and customs of national races." One of the duties and powers of the ministry created by the law is "making arrangements for the promotion and propagation of the *sasana* [Buddhist religion] in the Development Areas." The SLORC has also created or revived several Buddhist missionary universities, which send out monks to proselytize, often with the assistance of military force, in ethnic minority areas. It has also renewed the tradition of monastic teaching for primary level children, and during the early months of 1997 when all primary schools were closed, these were the only educational establishments available in many areas. Recently, Catholic families in Taunggyi have been encouraged to send their children to monastic schools, the encouragement being that though they might not get a better education that way, it could be the only education open to them. In this climate, then, it is risky though not impossible for individual monks or monasteries to cooperate with NGOs, and the *sangha* as a whole is viewed by the government as yet another means of social control, one it is unlikely to let go of.

CONCLUSION

Overall, the prospect for the development of civil society in Burma is grim. Even without the military government and its pervasive military intelligence agents, it would take a major shift in ways of thinking and working, starting from educational methods, for civil society to really take root and prosper. Fundamental to this process would be a relaxing of media censorship. However, the Burmese people have always lived with draconian laws, and have quite often found ways around them. In a situation where there is no civil society, and where the West is deeply distrusted, throwing money at the problems won't help. If all the outside world seeks to do is to support and encourage through training and technical assistance those individuals, families, and organizations that do come forward with social development projects, it will be doing the best it can.

NOTES

1. These last developments are important for international NGOs, UN agencies, and even embassies which have traditionally relied on the use of satellite links to avoid the pervasive government tapping of telephone lines.

2. More recently, U Saw Oo Reh, the NLD MP for Loikaw in the Karenni state, was arrested early last year for having written papers during the election campaign in 1989–90 which discussed the issue of federalism.

3. E.g., Myanmar Maternal and Child Welfare Association (MMCWA), whose vice president is the wife of SLORC secretary one, Lt. Gen. Khin Nyunt. Despite this, the MMCWA was said to have a degree of autonomy at the local level—until recently when it was reported that every chairperson at township and village levels is now always the wife of the Township or Village Peace and Development Council chairman.

4. Many of the groups and associations which emerged in 1988 were revivals of pre-1962 groups and organizations which were first formed during the fight for independence in the 1930s. The groups used the language and insignia of these old associations, including most memorably the fighting peacock chosen as the symbol of the student unions, which was first used by Aung San in the 1930s. While this suggested that these groups had a contiguous history, in the intervening years of military rule most had died out rather than gone "underground."

5. This is not the notorious Declaration 1/90 which required all elected members of parliament to sign their agreement with the government's declaration that the election was intended not to produce a new parliament, but rather a constituent assembly to write a new constitution under which new elections would be held and power transferred.

6. Rohingyas are not a recognized ethnic minority under the 1982 Citizenship Law, and usually cannot prove residence in Burma by all ancestors from 1824 onwards, as required by that law. In fact, the law was specifically designed to refuse Rohingyas citizenship (see "Burma/ Bangladesh, Rohingya Muslims: Ending a Cycle of Exodus?" *HRW*/Asia, September 1996).

7. Place of residence as described in Article 13 of the Universal Declaration of Human Rights and Article 12 of the International Covenant on Civil and Political Rights.

8. These policies echo the 1958–60 policies of the military Caretaker Government under Gen. Ne Win, when tens of thousands of urban "squatters" were forcibly moved to new townships.

9. This whole process bears a striking resemblance to the way in which the constitutional assembly (the National Convention) delegates were selected, and the running of the convention since then. The SLORC has done very little which the military hasn't done before.

10. For further details, see Tin Maung Maung Than, "Sangha Reforms and Renewal of Sasana in Myanmar: Historical Trends and Contemporary Practice" in Trevor Ling, ed., *Buddhist Trends in South East Asia*.

"AXE-HANDLES OR WILLING MINIONS?": INTERNATIONAL NGOS IN BURMA

MARC PURCELL

The issue of how international non-governmental organizations (INGOs) should approach operating in Burma is a thorny one. This was particularly so in the early 1990s when they first entered Burma, and again in 1998, after Aung San Suu Kyi called for INGOs not to operate in Burma. In the early nineties, many development workers and the expatriate democracy movement felt that an INGO presence provided the State Law and Order Restoration Council (SLORC)—now renamed the State Peace and Development Council (SPDC)[1]—with legitimacy. Warnings were sounded: INGOs would fall prey to the junta's manipulation; aid would be stolen and sold to profit the government; INGOs would be used in propaganda and meaningful development would not reach those it was intended for. INGOs would become "willing minions" (to use the junta's terminology) executing its agendas. INGOs have been urged by Aung San Suu Kyi and many expatriate democracy activists, to take as their priority the large refugee populations in neighboring countries who are the most visible and accessible victims of the junta's misrule.

Despite the heat of the debate in the early nineties, some fifteen INGOs entered Burma and more continued to arrive to explore the environment (some have subsequently withdrawn).[2] What has their experience been? As Burma approaches its thirty-fifth year of military rule, what are the issues for INGOs wanting to work with Burmese inside Burma? What possibilities could be explored for facilitating the growth of civil society? What attitude should INGOs adopt towards the democracy movement inside Burma? This paper examines these questions, with a focus on INGO experience. It will:

- outline a theoretical model for understanding the variety of INGOs and how their approach to operating in Burma might be categorized;
- review the debate in 1991–2 about INGOs entering Burma;
- consider the realities of the INGO experience in Burma and the substance of accusations of manipulation by the junta;
- outline the difficulties of working with government-controlled partners and NGOs;
- consider the realities of reaching ethnic communities inside Burma;
- consider INGOs' responses to the NLD's policies on aid; and
- conclude with some suggestions for a revised INGO approach to operating inside Burma.

The information presented is based on discussions with INGO and UN personnel from inside and outside Burma and opposition spokespeople from the National Coalition Government of the Union of Burma. The information presented is meant to be indicative of an evolving situation as seen in early 1998. The author apologizes for any inaccuracies in the information presented. An appendix includes a brief summary of health data for Burma, to explain the humanitarian imperative that INGOs are attempting to respond to.

GENERATIONS OF NGO STRATEGIES

The development theorist David Kortens distinguishes between four different "generations" of NGO strategies.[3] Kortens traces an evolutionary pattern from traditional relief activities towards greater involvement in catalyzing larger institutional and policy changes for social development. Such a "generation" approach is a tool rather than a hierarchy, and the point has been made elsewhere that many development agencies attempt to span the first three generations in the scope of their work.[4]

First Generation Strategy

First generation INGO's strategies involve the direct delivery of services to meet an immediate deficiency or shortage experienced by the beneficiary population, such as food, health care, and shelter. The focus is welfare based with a strong emphasis on logistical management. Many of the agencies on the Thai-Burma border, such as the Burma Border Consortium and Medecins Sans Frontieres–France, originally had this focus of providing food and health assistance and, in addition, were constrained from education and infrastructure work by their agreements with the Thai government. In Burma too, many agencies such as Medecins San Frontieres–Holland entered the country with a clear humanitarian relief focus, providing such programs as immunization which targeted populations and providing curative assistance—although these services have changed over time.

Second Generation Strategy

Second generation strategies attempt to develop the capacities of communities to better meet their own needs through self-reliant local action. INGOs working in this field commonly identify themselves as development INGOs. Activities might involve initiating village self-help actions with the development of health committees to carry out preventative health, digging wells, or improving agricultural practices. The concepts of "sustainable development" and "community development" are crucial to their modus operandi and there are different emphases placed on the "empowerment" of people. It is important to note that second generation approaches often grow out of first generation NGO responses to humanitarian need. The projects are often micro-focused on villages or sub-groups such as women and limited to short funding cycles tied to government donors. The role of the development NGO is to be a mobilizer and to assist in dissolving social inertia. Some critics argue that such a developmental approach inherently creates a dependent community. Further, such an approach requires countless repetitions to bring about broad social change.

Many of the agencies that have entered Burma—World Concern, World Vision, Save the Children Fund UK—are attempting to use these second generation strategies. They may incorporate first generation strategies into their work too. The approach is broad, from working with government departments and government-organized NGOs

(GONGOs) in areas such as capacity building in community health, to identifying needs and working with grassroots communities with as little government input as possible. World Concern, for example, operates in Kachin state with the Kachin Baptist Convention as its local partner and focuses on training village women in basic health diagnosis skills. Many smaller INGOs on the Thai-Burma border that don't have an agreement with the Thai authorities attempt this kind of education and capacity-building work—sometimes across the border.

Currently most INGOs in Burma are struggling with the constraints that the SPDC places upon this work, particularly in terms of sustainability. One INGO explained:

> Myanmar is extremely bureaucratic, and following the mode of government since 1962 there are few people who fully understand the mindset of "bottom up" participatory development which is so important to NGOs working in community development.[5]

Second generation strategies can actively target government and institutional oppression, but none of the agencies currently in Burma do this. The Thai-based Burma Border Consortium plays a strong but discreet advocacy role on behalf of refugees with the Thai government and international governments. This is despite the fact that it predominantly uses first generation strategies of humanitarian assistance for aiding refugee communities.

Third Generation Strategy

Third generation NGO strategies are focused on sustainable systems development. They look beyond the individual community and seek changes in specific policies and institutions at local, national, and global levels. The strategies aim to produce a supportive national or international development system and aim at working with national agencies "to help them orientate their polices and work modes in ways that strengthen broadly based local control over resources."[6] These initiatives arose out of frustration with second generation strategies where the benefit to a community may be dependent on a continued NGO presence and availability of donor subsidies. Moreover the limited coverage of NGO programs to clusters of villages and hostility of national institutions to sustainable community development meant that broad social development seemed very distant. Kortens elaborates:

> The underlying theory of third generation strategies is grounded in the assumption that local inertia is sustained by structures that centralise control of resources, keep essential services from reaching the poor, and maintain systems of corruption and exploitation. Creating the necessary changes often depends on working simultaneously to build the capacity of the people to make demands on the system and working to build alliances with enlightened power holders in support of action that makes the system more responsive to people.[7]

There has been a concerted push by some INGOs to develop this form of macro-level change on the issue of HIV/AIDS, and they work closely with the staff of the Burmese Department of Health to develop national strategies. However, those working on the HIV/AIDS epidemic have realized the limitations of a national approach, as any potential action is subordinated to the imperatives of the political system and also the personal vagaries of the (recently removed) minister of health who refused to acknowledge that Burma had an HIV/AIDS crisis. To be truly effective, a macro approach needs to go further and tackle the dysfunctional nature of military government. Such a broad strategy accords with the position advocated by the National League for Democracy (NLD) and the many critics in the Burmese community of INGOs in Burma who urge that INGO programs reach all of the people, not just those in favor with the government; that development must tackle the systemic nature of oppression in Burma if it is to be meaningful; and that cooperation with an oppressive government and its agencies can fatally compromise meaningful development.

Development INGOs in Burma feel that while this may be the ultimate goal, they are constrained by the SPDC's scrutiny from this approach. Their focus has been to position themselves inside Burma; address community health problems to the fullest extent possible; learn about the country; build up relationships and be in a good position to carry out more participatory development when conditions change. Many INGOs have worked under restrictive conditions in Thailand in the late 1970s, in Cambodia (1988–1993), and in Vietnam (1991–1997), experiencing a change in operating conditions as the government relaxed its control and they were able to reach communities more effectively. This experience informs their current activities and raises hopes for community development in the future, when devolution of power arrives in Burma.

Fourth Generation Strategy

The fourth generation strategy, according to Kortens, is an outcome of dissatisfaction with institutional resistance or hostility to third generation NGO initiatives. Fourth generation theorists argue that INGOs must look beyond "repair work" and adopt a decentralized action towards development and become "facilitators of a global people's development movement." How does this high-sounding rhetoric align with reality? How do INGOs move towards fourth generation strategies? Kortens specifies that INGOs must seek to facilitate "social movements" which mobilize people for social change. He describes them thus:

> Social movements have a special quality. They are driven not by budgets or organisational structures, but rather by ideas, by a vision of a better world. They move more on social energy rather than money. The vision mobilises independent action by countless individuals across national boundaries, all supporting a shared ideal. Participants in successful movements collaborate in continuously shifting networks and coalitions. They may quarrel over ideological issue and tactics. But where they have been successful, their efforts have generated a reinforcing synergy.[8]

Examples of social movements are the women's movement, and movements in the areas of peace, environment, consumer affairs, and human rights. The trade union movement, with its emphasis on labor rights, is one of the oldest of these social movements. Kortens believes that "development" has not generally been viewed as a social movement and development INGOs are not attuned to fully working as facilitators of social movements, although clearly efforts have been made in the areas of women and the environment in recent years.

In the case of Burma, the struggle for democracy, ethnic rights, and respect for human rights by the Burmese, is developing into an international social movement. The arrival of an estimated ten thousand democracy activists and students on the Thai-Burma border and in other countries, in 1988, has led to alliances with the ethnic peoples to change the political system of Burma. This blend of democratic, federal sentiment has had a symbiotic effect of increasing international awareness about the democracy struggle and abuses against ethnic peoples. A wide range of advocacy INGOs and people's organizations have focused on different aspects of the political situation in Burma and the movement for social change such as human rights organizations (e.g. Amnesty International and Human Rights Watch–Asia) women's organizations (e.g. the Indigenous Women's Center, NGO support for Burmese delegates to Beijing Women's NGO Conference), ethnic rights advocates and development bodies (e.g. the Karen Human Rights Group and the Burma Relief Center), and the environment movement (e.g. Green November 32, Earthrights International). The Burma Border Consortium recognize the importance of advocacy and employ elements of this strategy in their information role and lobbying based in Thailand.

Crucial to the success of social movements is the flow of information. The development of the Burmanet e-mail news group dramatically increased international awareness and the information produced by organizations located in Thailand spreads out across the world. Burma advocacy centers exist in nine European countries, the US, Canada, Australia and Japan. They reinforce and bring consistency and depth to international awareness of the nature of life under the Burmese military.[9] They foster an impetus for change.[10]

If we accept that the struggle for democracy in and around Burma is a social movement, then meaningful development is not accomplished by an exclusive focus on first, second or third generation development strategies. Rather it would entail development agencies undertaking advocacy and resourcing those bodies which practice advocacy. It could incorporate second generation community development, capacity building, and institutional strengthening, but in the context of an overall strategy of facilitating and strengthening the broader social movement for change.

The fourth generation approach has yet to be fully explored by INGOs inside Burma and by many outside Burma. It would necessitate a rethink of the roles and limited foci many INGOs have in their work. At the end of this paper, I will make some general comments about models for INGOs wanting to facilitate a fourth generation approach to development in Burma. The following section provides a brief historical account of how development INGOs came to enter Burma.

THE AID DEBATE

Prior to 1988, as a result of the autarkic nature of the Ne Win junta, the lack of civil society, and the isolation of Burma, INGOs had little relationship with the Burmese Government. There were funding relationships between INGOs such as World Vision, OXFAM–UK, and western churches with Burmese church partners, Burma Red Cross, and a few local organizations such as hospitals. Many of these relationships and bilateral Official Development Aid (ODA) lapsed in the wake of the 1988 uprising and the 1990 election. INGOs effectively boycotted Burma.

The impetus for the debate as to whether INGOs should reenter Burma came from a number of changes. Firstly, the SLORC made it clear in 1989 that accompanying their more open policy to foreign investment was a willingness to have humanitarian organizations work with the Burmese people. Secondly, UN bodies such as UNICEF entered Burma and called for INGOs to enter en masse and take advantage of the changed conditions. The 1992 paper "Possibilities for a United Nations Peace and Development Initiative for Myanmar" by James Grant, the executive director of UNICEF, had the catalytic effect of drawing attention to the appalling social indices of underdevelopment in Burma and stirring up a debate as to whether agencies should enter.[11] (See appendix.)

Amidst controversy, two INGOs originally working with refugees in Thailand, Medecins Sans Frontieres (MSF)–Holland, and World Vision International opted to enter Burma to explore opportunities in 1989–92.

In response to these events, the International Council of Voluntary Agencies (ICVA), an association of INGOs, decided to send a mission to Burma in 1993, led by their chairman, Russell Rollason.[12] The purpose of the two-week mission was several-fold:[13]

- to assess the humanitarian situation in Burma;
- to meet local Burmese INGOs;

- to discuss with the government and agencies mechanisms for INGOs operating in Burma; and
- to assess the situation of Burmese refugees in Thailand and Bangladesh.

Amongst other things, the ICVA mission sought and was denied an interview with (the then imprisoned) Aung San Suu Kyi, but did meet with opposition groups in Thailand and considered the human rights situation. It found a strong moral argument for trade sanctions and called for an international arms embargo. However, it did not recommend aid sanctions—on the basis that the Burmese people would suffer and that there were opportunities to slowly change the practices of the regime.[14] The report portrayed a humanitarian crisis in all social and economic areas in Burma and focused particularly on the emerging HIV/AIDS pandemic. While necessarily an overview, the report made a valuable contribution by bringing together a snapshot of the human cost of years of military rule and the neglect of social services and the entrenchment of poverty.[15] The report stirred up strong debate. It was the mission's nine-point guidelines for INGOs desiring to enter Burma, and by implication the mission's endorsement for INGOs to enter Burma, that overshadowed the other recommendations and was controversial amongst the expatriate Burmese community and with others.[16]

The Australia Burma Council, for instance, argued that aid should be targeted to the Thai-Burma border, that aid inside Burma could not be accurately monitored, that a resumption of aid would give the SLORC international credibility and that there was evidence that increasing international pressure from the UN was beginning to affect the regime.[17] Saw Ba Thin, the general secretary of the Karen National Union, and Jack Dunford, the chairperson of the Committee to Co-ordinate Services to the Displaced Persons in Thailand (CCSDPT) argued strongly that it was not the right time for INGOs to enter Burma because of the ongoing conflict on the Thai-Burma border and the steadily increasing number of refugees.[18] They recommended aid should be channeled to the refugees and that further exploration of cross-border assistance be made.[19]

In response to these arguments, Roger Walker, the policy adviser of World Vision Australia (WVA) made a passionate plea that the political arguments condemning the SLORC shouldn't blind people to the social costs of denying aid:[20]

> I do not intend to convey an impression that World Vision regards human rights or democratic reform as unimportant; they are important; but they should not be a cause for the poor to be punished for the acts of others. The growing child cannot wait until the right government comes along or until the war has ended. There is a principle that the suffering child has a right to development—to health, to education. They cannot wait until tomorrow.[21]

Russell Rollason of ICVA, also argued against INGOs ignoring the humanitarian needs inside Burma.[22] He also relied on an argument of not "punishing the poor" and pointed out that valuable time was being lost. He asked:

> Is the time right for NGOs to consider involvement in Burma? I believe the time is right. The choice is "now or wait." It is three years since Aung San Suu Kyi won the free and fair election in Burma and the SLORC rejected the people's democratic choice. In those three years trade with the SLORC has increased significantly, as have, regrettably, arms sales to the SLORC, yet little has been done to build links with people and NGOs in Burma. NGO involvement will open up new flows of information, broaden people to people links, offer solidarity and draw increased attention to the silent emergency in Burma.[23]

Though not all INGOs were persuaded by the "human need" or "now is the time" arguments, the result of this debate was that many agencies were persuaded to assist the refugees on the Thai-Burma border. Others facilitated small advocacy NGOs and initiatives to promote the democracy movement and ethnic groups.[24] Opposition to INGOs operating in Burma from the politically active Burmese community, and some INGO workers has remained strong since then.[25] The National Coalition Government of the Union of Burma urged development agencies to focus on the "external situation" of refugees, trafficking of women and HIV/AIDS (despite the internal causes of these problems) and provide training to those in the "liberated areas" of Burma.[26]

Drawing on this community concern, a number of useful guidelines were produced for INGOs considering operating inside Burma.[27]

INGO APPROACHES

Despite INGO focus on refugees and the civil and political human rights situation inside Burma, a shift has occurred amongst donor governments who maintained restrictions on ODA.[28] Some INGOs who did want to enter Burma to respond to the humanitarian needs there, lobbied donor governments for funds.[29] These new government donor and UN funding windows for INGOs were designed to meet vulnerable sections of the Burmese populace and to be less controversial, in that they were aimed at cross-cutting issues. The battle against HIV/AIDS, it was considered, could not wait for a change in the political order. Moreover HIV/AIDS in Burma, if left unaddressed, represented a glaring hole in regional strategies to combat its spread in the Asian region. As a result of the social needs in Burma and new donor funding windows, some INGOs went in to explore the situation.[30] The situation they found was bleak.

All government statistics on health and other social indices were incomplete and questionable. UN surveys gave the most accurate, if incomplete picture. Burma's most immediate needs were in the health sector. The government health system was extensive but inadequate for the size of the population and suffered structural flaws and a minuscule budget in relation to needs. Propaganda had often taken the place of substantial medical services, i.e. the system existed on paper in some places but not in practice.[31] The assistance provided by UNICEF, UNDP, and other UN bodies are the only bulwarks against the effective collapse of the government health and education programs.[32]

These UN bodies, acting on the macro level of management and assessment, are now increasingly looking to INGOs to act as implementing bodies for development programs at a community level.

A general breakdown of INGO approaches to the health crisis in Burma is useful:

- *Curative medical approach:* Action Contre la Faim (ACF); The Association of Medical Doctors of Asia for Better Quality Life for a Better Future (AMDA); Mèdecins du Monde (MdM);

Medecins Sans Frontieres (MSF–Holland);

- *Health education approach:* Australian Red Cross (ARC, withdrew Feb. '97); World Concern; World Vision Myanmar (WVM); Association Francois Xavier Bagnoud (AFXB); Adventist Development and Relief Agency (ADRA); CARE Myanmar; MdM; MSF–Holland;
- *Income generation/livelihood approach:* (AFXB); CARE Myanmar; Groupe de Recherche et d'Echanges Technologiques (GRET); OISCA International; World Vision Myanmar;
- *Multi-sectoral integrated community development approach:* World Vision Myanmar; CARE Myanmar; ADRA;
- *Family planning approach:* Marie Stopes International (MSI); Population Services International (PSI);
- *Child focused approach:* Save the Children Fund UK (SCF UK); Save the Children Fund USA (SCF USA); World Vision Myanmar; CARE Myanmar;
- Unclassified: Bridge Asia Japan (BAJ); PACT.

PROBLEMS AND PRACTICALITIES

Most INGOs wishing to operate in Burma must have an agreement with the junta. The exceptions are Red Cross national organizations, which can sign directly with Myanmar Red Cross; and a few INGOs which went into Arakan State under the UNHCR mandate for the Rohingya repatriation. The SPDC does not encourage this latter model, however.

Memorandums of Understanding (MOUs) allow INGOs to operate inside Burma and are generally the result of lengthy and frustrating negotiations with government ministries, such as the Ministry of Health. There is no central body for MOUs. INGOs must approach the junta's Foreign Affairs Committee made up of senior SPDC officers, such as Lieutenant General Khin Nyunt, secretary of the SPDC and head of Military Intelligence, and General Than Shwe, prime minister and chief of defense, before final approval is given by the Cabinet. INGOs must have a representative from a ministry make their case to the committee. By the nature of authority in Burma, it helps to have good, sympathetic contacts within the government to facilitate the process. Because of the personalized nature of governmental rule, there is a degree of "capriciousness" and INGOs are dependent on whims of officials in this process and for the final decision.[33] One agency noted that:

> The top leaders in Government are constantly reassessing the roles of NGOs in Myanmar and any organization operating in country must therefore be adaptive and have a high tolerance for ambiguity.[34]

One agency noted that there appeared to be a de facto, two-stage process developing of, firstly, being permitted to register a presence in Burma, (by establishing an office, obtaining a fax license, hiring local staff) and then a delay occurs—sometimes a wait of between twelve and twenty-four months before projects or MOUs can be undertaken—while SPDC observes the agency. Secondly, the MOU process of negotiation takes place with the relevant ministries before final approval by the Foreign Affairs Committee.[35]

Another agency noted that there seems to be a freeze on western INGOs. Two INGOs had been rejected from obtaining MOUs in 1996 and allegedly the government had a preference for Asian INGOs which were considered more politically quiescent. The Ministry of Health has now five years' experience in dealing with INGOs and is generally on the side of INGO project proposals. However, the Ministry of Health is relatively low in the SPDC's pecking order, as are other non-income generating ministries, such as Basic Education and Social Welfare, that INGOs commonly want to work with.

Memorandums of Understanding are relatively standard umbrella documents, which generally state the following:

- Permission to establish a presence in Burma and permission to open an office.
- A government ministry (generally the Ministry of Health) is named to act as an NGO counterpart and assist with visas, IDD telephone lines, clearance of importation of equipment and supplies, internal transport, establishment of a bank account and any other assistance.
- The counterpart ministry will help with liaison with other government ministries.
- Each NGO project will be implemented subject to a specific written project agreement with the Ministry of Health and be implemented though local authorities.

- The ministry will grant the NGO the same kind of approvals enjoyed by other NGOs.
- The NGO will be exempt from government taxes on imports of supplies and equipment, personal effects, and salaries for foreign staff.
- NGO staff are allowed to use the local kyat or FEC currency rate.
- The NGO retains financial responsibility for the projects.
- The NGO provides an annual report to the ministry.
- The NGO will train local staff so projects are sustainable.
- The NGO will develop the capacities of Burmese people and so will collaborate with local organizations.
- The NGO will undertake ". . . that its representative and personnel shall not interfere with the political and religious affairs of Myanmar and shall abide by the laws and regulations of Myanmar."

POLITICAL RESTRICTIONS

INGOs point out that, theoretically, such MOUs allow more latitude to undertake their own activities than similar arrangements in countries like Vietnam. However, the last stipulation on political activity is obeyed by INGOs. INGOs instructed staff to avoid attending NLD activities, including Aung San Suu Kyi's historic weekend talks (banned in September 1996). Such unofficial discouragement has extended (until recently) to communication with Daw Aung San Suu Kyi. The separation between public/work roles and private life does not exist in Burma and INGOs have fallen in with this culture by self-monitoring all their actions so they will not be judged harshly by the SPDC. INGOs believed in 1996 that the SPDC viewed INGOs as having too much autonomy and was moving to control their independence. One agency wrote:

> The government is highly concerned with control and internal security and is often extremely cautious about the purpose and presence of international NGOs. Therefore international NGOs . . . . who have chosen to work inside Myanmar have needed patience, perseverance and great care in order to operate in a way that does not compromise the necessary

ethical standards, and quality of project implementation, in such a politically constrained context.[36]

Another NGO felt that INGOs had to work under a "cloak of caution." INGOs were:

> . . . reluctant to meet with opposition parties and certain ethnic leaders because such meetings might jeopardise approval of projects, signing of MOUs, or permission to work in certain parts of the country (i.e.) the border areas . . . staff are cautious of what is said because it could be reported back to the SLORC.[37]

There was increasing surveillance and most INGOs have had all their mail opened. In 1997 two established INGOs were ordered to leave on the whim of the minister of health, but one was able to effectively lobby Khin Nyunt to have the order rescinded and the other continues to operate by having local staff and a foreign development worker enter regularly on a tourist visa. The effect of this SPDC warning will be to increase the sense of vulnerability for all INGOs and make them keep their heads down.

Some INGOs state that the local Law and Order Restoration Councils initially watched their activities closely, but as time went by this scrutiny was reduced. They implemented their programs as they wished and reached their target communities. A few INGO workers differed and maintained that the SPDC would allow nothing outside their control and really only wanted INGO money but not their presence.

INGOs in Burma do not openly criticize the government for bearing the prime responsibility for bringing about the continuing decline in social and economic welfare. Most do not search for means to report on other human rights abuses such as torture, forced labor, and persecution of the NLD, but this is not to say that it has not been attempted. INGOs argue that it is not in their primary mandate to do these things and, secondly, by drawing attention to highly sensitive issues like forced labor or military expenditure, they will raise the ire of the SPDC and damage the viability of worthwhile programs. INGO workers in Burma concede that the work that they do is a drop in the ocean compared to the scale of need, but all disagree strongly with the suggestion that nothing can be done to improve people's health, or that nothing should be attempted while the military remains in power.

INGOs claim that the junta has not made use of the INGOs' presence for propaganda purposes. Nevertheless the risks are there. One former INGO worker commented:

> I was asked to accompany a team for the first training (in HIV/AIDS prevention) at Dawei, a coastal town in the south where foreigners rarely go. The opening ceremony was dominated by the regional SLORC commander and appeared on State television that night. Subsequently I quietly avoided being seen or photographed in the company of high SPDC officials, though had to meet many officials in the course of the project work over the next year and a half. The training session went well.[38]

INGO COMMUNICATION

INGOs meet regularly on technical issues such as HIV/AIDS and have held monthly general information meetings. There are only a small number of INGOs in Burma compared to other countries in the region and the disparate sizes of INGOs and the varied areas and approaches to programming haven't leant themselves to extensive inter-agency cooperation. Moreover, some believe that there is an apparent lack of solidarity amongst the INGO community. They did not (openly at least) rally to defend those INGOs who recently had their MOUs canceled. Nor have they advocated on the part of those INGOs who have been waiting for over two years to have their MOUs approved.

Until recently INGOs were reluctant to present the work that they were doing in Burma to international forums lest their presence in Burma be criticized or the information they present be used to attack the SPDC and jeopardize their work.[39] They feel somewhat embattled by the advocacy NGOs outside Burma. Earlier hopes for an increased flow of information from INGOs about conditions inside Burma have not born much fruit. This was particularly noticeable in 1996–7, with the lack of news about the recent floods and the fate of internally displaced people. While World Vision, MSF–Holland, World Concern, Save the Children Fund UK and CARE have all recently participated in some

Burma NGO meetings outside Burma, many other INGOs in Burma have not.

Their absence is noticeable in international forums such as the Burma Donor's Secretariat, which comprises agencies which are focused on the refugee situation in Burma's neighbors, but with whom much could be shared and learnt for mutual benefit. They do not attend the Thai based BBC information meetings (unless they are outgoing staff) because of its advocacy content and Thai location. As a result of this gulf between INGOs inside and outside Burma, there is a lost opportunity to have dialogue and build up a new understanding, particularly on technical issues such as education or the cross-border nature of HIV/ AIDS.

Theft of Aid

The issue of aid being taken by the SPDC and sold on the black market has not occurred to the extent feared because INGOs concentrated their services in the area of training rather than hard resources or cash. Nevertheless, as one aid worker revealed, a small percentage of aid in his agency (in the order of 5 percent) does go astray, but this is similar to the level in other countries. (He did not specify whether this was due to a problem with the junta or the INGOs local staff). When Myanmar Red Cross entered a period of renegotiation with Australian Red Cross, the head of the Myanmar Red Cross allegedly requested—and received—the hand-over of vehicles owned by Australian Red Cross. Some parts of the government have taken advantage of the highly over-valued exchange rate (officially US$1: 6 kyat, unofficially US$1:300 kyat) to try and suck dollars out of INGOs. INGOs who have signed with the Ministry of Health operate on a local currency (kyat) basis in most areas, but when it comes to paying for internal airfares and other transport, the Ministry of Transport has recently decided not recognize the Ministry of Health MOU and insists in payment in US$ or the vastly overvalued Foreign Exchange Certificates (FECs). INGOs have not been successful negotiating around this lack of respect for their MOUs.

A related issue is that some INGOs consider themselves being treated rapaciously by Burmese who rent properties for offices and dwellings; exorbitant rents are the norm. Several INGO workers raised the issue of value for money: did the ratio of expenditure on running costs (particularly the long setting-up time required) outweigh the relatively small expenditure on programs and the actual success of those programs? Another question raised by an INGO worker was about the depth of relationship and understanding that INGO personnel have with the Burmese communities when INGO offices and homes are located in the most expensive part of Rangoon surrounded by senior military and government officials (and the homes of the NLD leaders).

LIAISON WITH GOVERNMENT-ORGANIZED NGOS

Government-organized NGOs (GONGOs) are parastatal bodies, ostensibly created for social welfare purposes, with officially sanctioned national networks and heavily influenced by the SPDC's agendas. They include the Myanmar Maternal Child Welfare Association, Myanmar Medical Association, Myanmar Red Cross Society, Myanmar Anti-Narcotic Association, Auxiliary Fire Brigade, Parent Teachers Associations and the Myanmar Nurses Association. The Union Solidarity and Development Association (USDA) is an inchoate political party for the army's future political ambitions but has also been erroneously identified by some INGOs as a local NGO.

INGOs will remain attracted to the GONGO's extensive networks as they desire local partners, and have been influenced by the junta's (and in some cases, embassy's) preferences that they work through GONGOs.[40] Not all INGOs work with GONGOs however. Some like MSF–Holland have an independent system of health clinics and avoid much contact with the government and its bodies, while others have engaged with GONGOs at times but mostly focus on their own programs with communities. Initially INGOs ignored the political nature of GONGOs and the ramifications of working with them in their eagerness to have implementing partners. Most based their relationships with GONGOs on inadequate assessments made in the early to mid 1990s when less was known about their political nature.

GONGOs are often led by senior officials with military backgrounds and their effectiveness seems to vary according to the personality of the individual in charge. They can be obstructionist, winding back programs, failing to start new ones, monopolizing resources for their purposes, or denying the extent of social or health problems. Some believe that Myanmar Red Cross is the most recalcitrant GONGO. MRC's president (recently removed in the fallout from the creation of the SPDC) halted meaningful programming on HIV/AIDS and insisted that staff participate in pro-SLORC Union Solidarity Development Association (USDA) rallies.[41] Some foreign medical professionals had praise for the current leadership of the Myanmar Nurses Association as an effective body.

The political agendas of the regime influence these bodies. In the wake of seven years of persecution of the Rohingyas in Arakan state, the Myanmar Maternal & Child Welfare Association has commenced a family planning program in Arakan state where "there were many Muslims."[42] All GONGO personnel are regularly mobilized to participate in USDA rallies (as are other citizens and local NGO staff). In terms of professional capacity, the GONGOs have highly trained personnel. Institutionally however, they are conservative and sometimes inactive.

INGO have held training courses aimed at raising the awareness of the leadership of the government-organized NGOs such as the Myanmar Maternal & Child Welfare Association (MMCWA) as well as more independent church based social welfare bodies and the YMCA and YWCA. INGOs concluded that it was difficult to produce a change in thinking or organizational culture in GONGOs. Nevertheless, the training can have some positive effect on their recipients. During 1994–95, UNICEF, World Vision and Save the Children Fund UK coordinated and organized a number of workshops for MMCWA to try and assist this process of understanding the nature of NGOs and strategic planning. World Vision noted:

> The character of these GONGOs is often very different at the township or ward level from the central level. They can also vary greatly from one area to another, depending upon the individual members in each place . . . Like many future uncertainties in Myanmar it is not clear whether there is potential for any of these GONGOs to develop into more genuine local NGOs, although there may be signs that this could happen with MMCWA.[43]

Initially such training entailed that INGOs were working with the better-off in society and some Burmese view those leading the GONGOs—even at a village level—as opportunists. However there is a clear sense that it is effective for INGOs to work with, and train, individual GONGOs members. Indeed, at village and district level of GONGOs, ordinary members of the Myanmar Maternal & Child Welfare Association and Myanmar Red Cross have a high degree of enthusiasm and welcomed the training, resources, and presence of INGO programs. INGOs point out that GONGO members often wear several hats: they may be local government members, but equally they could be health professionals or ethnic community leaders, members of local churches or even NLD supporters (on the quiet). The point is made that individuals in the community have no choice but to work for their community through government-sanctioned GONGOs. INGOs now feel they have more knowledge about communities and are more confident that they can target people genuinely interested in receiving training whether they are GONGO members or not.

Local NGOS and Churches

There are a range of local NGOs and church bodies which despite laws which confine them to religious activities, manage to operate a diverse range of programs of varying quality.[44] Most bodies span the spectrum of conservative, but important welfare/humanitarian relief activities, to more interesting community development initiatives. Most of the local NGOs are closely interrelated with churches. However individuals doing development activities often cited frustration with the conservatism or lack of interest of church boards, the lack of technical understanding and the constraints the government put on their activities. Having survived decades of Ne Win's isolationism, churches and the few local NGOs are cautiously sending young members overseas to be trained in aspects of community development and tentatively expanding their welfare/development activities.

For INGOs, the constraints and the strengths of the churches and the local NGOs are intertwined:

- Charity predominates over community development approaches.
- The evangelical nature of the churches is overt, with a Christian tenor pervading many NGO activities, which is problematic in a Buddhist country.
- Organizations are conducting extensive training in community

health and sending small groups and individuals abroad for community development training.

- Churches and individual bishops are the only viable conduit of providing emergency aid to internally displaced people.
- Most programs are non-discriminatory in accessing all of the community, while some, such as school programs are intent on instilling a Christian education.
- The government will not register bodies such as the YMCA as NGOS, but monitors them under the Ministry of Home and Religious Affairs. This limits their ability to receive funds from overseas or to conduct in-country training with foreign experts.
- The churches are predominantly comprised of ethnic minorities who are located in Rangoon and the outlying ethnic states, rather than the predominantly ethnic Burman (and Buddhist) heartland.
- There are individuals within these bodies who are development orientated, are taking initiatives and who are aware of the limitations of their approaches and are interested in capacity building, training and exchanges.

THE CHANGING CONTEXT

From 1993, a number of changes have occurred inside Burma which affect how INGOS approach Burma. Between 1989 and 1996, a majority of ethnic insurgent groups have made ceasefires with the SPDC and some have called for aid and development assistance. Aung San Suu Kyi was released in June 1995 and has made it known, unofficially, that she wants INGOS to talk with the NLD about their programs in Burma and subsequently has called on INGOS to not enter Burma. What are the implications of these two changes?

Ethnic Minorities

The advent of ceasefires with ethnic insurgent communities is an important shift in the political culture of Burma away from armed conflict.[45] The corresponding calls of ethnic groups for development assistance need to be considered, not just by those agencies inside Burma, but those opponents of aid to Burma who have appeared to ignore the calls of ethnic groups (particularly non-insurgent organized ethnic peoples) for direct aid and development. Since 1989, when the SLORC took tactical advantage of the mutiny in the old Burma Communist Party to make a ceasefire with its ethnic Wa cadres, the trend has been towards ceasefires. Currently all the major ethnic groups except for the Karen National Union and the Rohingya Liberation Front have made ceasefires with the SPDC (the Karenni National People's Party ceasefire fell apart in June 1996). While these fall far short of political settlements and many ethnic grievances remain, they are a modus vivendi, recognition by ethnic leaderships that their peoples were exhausted from years of warfare. The guerrilla struggle was becoming increasingly untenable as the regional geopolitical situation changed and Burma's neighbors, particularly China and Thailand, switched from various forms of ideological and material support for the ethnic insurgents, to more lucrative bilateral arrangements with the new military junta eager for regional investment.

The most significant shift was the Kachin Independence Organization (KIO) taking its 8,000 troops into ceasefire in early 1994, causing considerable angst in the opposition ethnic/democracy grouping, the Democratic Alliance of Burma (DAB). As a result, the priorities for the KIO have changed. The Central Committee of the KIO issued a statement in August 1994:

> The current cease-fire agreement between the KIO and SLORC provides for an accelerated rate of infrastructure and economic development in Kachin State and adjoining sub-State. In as much as the SPDC has assumed responsibility for the development of the country, it is incumbent on each nationality to undertake its respective regions (sic) economic growth and overall advancement. Should local resources prove inadequate, the KIO will seek any avenue of assistance including outside help where available. The KIO urges SLORC to facilitate access to any and all who wish to actively help and participate in this urgent effort in much the same degree of urgency that the KIO has begun to solicit support from private, governments and NGOs from within and abroad.[46]

It is clear that the KIO is calling for INGO assistance and that they expect to have to develop their region themselves, not with aid from the junta, but with the junta facilitating outside assistance.

Subsequently, World Concern and TEAR Australia entered to work in Kachin state in 1994 in a MOU brokered by the Reverend Saboy Jum of the Kachin Baptist Convention and Khin Nyunt.

With the Mon ceasefire made in early 1996, the NMSP echoed the call of the Kachin for assistance. Similarly Karenni community leaders have called for development assistance lest their people resort to opium growing in the relative drug-free state.[47] In the light of these calls, the position that INGOs should not be in Burma at all becomes increasingly difficult to maintain. While individual agencies may chose to work with ethnic groups on the borders and provide necessarily limited cross-border assistance, to reach groups in the heart of Burma and to do more substantial health training, it is a reality that INGOs may need to negotiate a MOU with the SPDC.

A similar issue of providing aid to repatriated refugees arises. Since 1993 a fitful repatriation of some 260,000 Rohingya refugees from Bangladesh back into Arakan state has occurred. (Some 20,000 refugees remain in Bangladesh and many abuses are still occurring inside Arakan state, while UNHCR has been criticized for failing to live up to its own protection standards.) It seems untenable to argue that aid should be halted to the Rohingya which was willingly extended before they crossed back into Burma. The Rohingya in Arakan are served almost exclusively by INGO health clinics and UN food programs.

Another question for INGOs is whether their presence in any way reduces the oppressive conditions for repatriated ethnic communities. Some have argued that some moderation of SPDC persecution of the Rohingya has occurred in Arakan state because of the foreign INGO and UN presence. The problem is that there is nothing systematic or permanent about INGO presence and protection. Nevertheless, if INGOs have signed a MOU to work inside Burma, they may be in a better position to access repatriated communities, if and when the SPDC decides to allow access to them. Others argue that it is highly dangerous to assume that because any INGO has a presence in a particular state or region, that this necessarily provides protection.

The argument that INGOs should focus purely on the refugee situation on the borders also misses the plight of internally displaced people inside Burma (sometimes assessed as up to one million). The local churches in Burma are struggling to get assistance to internally displaced people in Karenni (Kayah) and Shan states which deserve more INGO resourcing.

Access to border areas is extremely difficult. A MOU is necessary not just with the Ministry of Health, for instance, but also an agreement with the Ministry of Border Area Development which has refused to allow access to INGOs so far. However INGOs have managed to establish an extensive network of health services in Arakan state and several have been permitted to extend health training focusing on HIV/AIDS into the high drug use, jade mining areas of Kachin state. Some INGOs have lobbied SPDC secretary one, Khin Nyunt, for access to the eastern border, but even after many months of representations the Border Ministry has refused this. INGO representations with the Foreign Affairs Committee will remain critical for any agency seeking to work in ceasefire territory.

The Democracy Movement

In early 1996, the NLD put its position on UN development programs to the UNDP in a letter from Aung San Suu Kyi. She argued that the UNDP, as an agency of the United Nations which had passed successive General Assembly resolutions calling for the junta to implement democratic reforms, should not be cooperating with the regime. Aung San Suu Kyi was critical of the way the implementation of UNDP projects were influenced by the local level military authorities, which excluded NLD supporters from local community bodies such as parent teacher associations. She argued that training programs are filled with representatives of township and village level officials, GONGOs, USDA, and other government-related organizations. Where were the community and NLD members in these processes? Aung San Suu Kyi made two recommendations to UNDP:

1. "Humanitarian aid should reach the right people in the right way, it should not be reserved for those who stand in favor with the authorities—a process which runs contrary to the promotion of justice";
2. "It is absolutely necessary for those providing humanitarian aid to work closely with the NLD—the duly elected representatives of the Burmese people."

As a result, UNDP are making more effort to use a grassroots development approach and are turning to INGOs to be implementing partners.

After Aung San Suu Kyi's release in June 1995, the NLD revived and began calling for dialogue with the junta. Earlier statements that there should be "no trade, aid or investment" with the junta remained, but there was an ambiguity on the issue of an INGO presence. Privately, Aung San Suu Kyi made it clear that she wanted INGOs to consult with the NLD. The INGO response to this call has been poor for reasons outlined earlier. In addition many western embassies advised INGOs not to risk discussion with the NLD, lest they lose their MOU or not be granted one. Agency staff are troubled by the issue, some feeling that they should explore ways of talking with the NLD, but others feel that the risk is too high; one conversation with "The Lady" might cost them and the communities they work amongst, their programs. Nevertheless some discreet INGO contacts with the NLD have been made and it seemed clear that the NLD is eager to learn about development, INGO programming, how they access communities and how their relationship with the SPDC operates on the ground.

By 1998, however, the NLD's position has seemed to move against condoning an INGO presence. It is worth quoting a series of selected excerpts from an interview with Aung San Suu Kyi by Denise Nicholls. When asked about her position on INGOs working in Burma, the Nobel laureate compared INGOs to UN agencies:[48]

> We don't think the time is right for NGOs to come in. It is very difficult, if not impossible, for NGOs to work without permission of the authorities. They really can't do it. Even the UN agencies find it difficult to resist the influence of the authorities. We are always afraid that they will be manipulated by the authorities, as some UN agencies have been.

Aung San Suu Kyi elaborated her position in further remarks:

> Q. Wouldn't smaller agencies do better because they would work with the communities?
> A. Frankly, they would be in a weaker position than the UN.
>
> Q. As distinct from the UN, international NGOs are used to working

with local communities, so doesn't that make them different from the UN?

A. They still have to work with the local area State Peace and Development Council. I doubt that any NGO would be given free association in any community. Even local SPDCs would try and get favors for their own people from such programs. How can an NGO be sure about who it is really helping?

Q. Is there any way NGOs can work with the NLD?

A. I'm afraid not. There is no way. We (the NLD) would be happy to cooperate with NGOs and to help make sure that everyone gets a fair share. But the authorities won't allow it.

Q. How then can international NGOs help?

A. Why don't these NGOs go to the Karen refugees on the border? There's plenty of need there. We (inside) really have to help ourselves.

Q. But the NGOs are already on the border. They are the people helping—the UN is not even present. Besides, there are 100,000 refugees, and 40 million Burmese.

A. It would only be a drop in the ocean. Helping a few thousand here or there. We want to create a system which will help everyone. It is far more important to change the political system in Burma.

For those agencies that have already established a presence in Burma, and for those contemplating doing so, there are important questions of ethical principle at stake. Firstly, INGOs must respect the difficult decision that Burmese democracy activists have made in respect of not giving aid to their people inside Burma, because it is based on their commitment, a well-thought-out strategy, and the suffering they have endured. Few would dispute the NLD's assessment that systemic change is required before poverty alleviation on a macro scale can be tackled.

In response, some INGOs may choose not to operate in Burma; they may decide to run programs on the Thai-Burma border as an alternative, or to defer programming on Burma until later (a common position). Some INGOs would disagree with the NLD's strategy to exclude aid. As humanitarian organizations they would place priority on people's immediate health needs. Burma is now approaching the highest rate of HIV/AIDS infection in Southeast Asia with an estimated 40,000 people. They point to the fact that many people would have been infected with the disease through ignorance if INGOs and UN agencies had not been running awareness programs this past half decade.

INGO personnel point out that some fifty international, Thai, and Burmese indigenous NGOs attempt to deal with several hundred thousand Burmese refugees and unofficial refugees in Thailand. Inside Burma, just fifteen NGOs attempt to run programs in a population of 44 million, a proportion that is patently inadequate. However those INGO programs affect the lives of dozens each day, hundreds over the months and thousands over the years. The consequence of INGO work is that some Burmese people survive in good health whereas they might have suffered unnecessary illness or even death. They argue that training Burmese people to identify common diseases and improve maternal and child health is highly valuable.

The question of breaking with the opinion of the NLD on the issue of aid is hard. It seems to be a case of two conflicting principles. Implicit in the NLD position is that by INGOs choosing not to deal with the junta, its demise will be hastened. The price to pay for this course of action is not responding to human needs inside Burma of which we are presently aware, and postponing assistance until a change in the political system allows for a wider and more enduring program of action. Some INGOs will assess the human cost of this strategy as too high. Both aims have inherently good motivations but a genuine tension arises in trying to follow both of them. To some extent, pursuing one must be at the expense of the other. There may be no solution to this dilemma except to live with it. However it is important to note that for INGOs to differ on the issue of aid with the NLD in no way prevents them offering solidarity to the NLD on a whole raft of other issues.

If INGOs claim to be impartial and yet have a MOU with a military dictatorship to work to some extent through its structures, then it is absolutely clear that they have made a political choice. Impartiality, if it is to be realized in these conditions, requires that INGOs should consult with all concerned stakeholders: the target community, and the elected leaders of the Burmese people—the NLD and SPDC. INGOs in Burma have readily resorted to the powerful argument of people in need to justify their presence in Burma. A similar moral imperative presses upon them not to dodge the call of Aung San Suu Kyi to discuss their projects.

INGOs, as exponents of the value of improving human life and bringing about social change, do have the ethical responsibility to consider whether they support the democracy and respect for human rights as represented by the NLD, and if they do, they must explore how to safely communicate with Aung San Suu Kyi and the NLD about their projects.

More broadly, INGOs must consider how their work facilitates what is the only real macro "development" in Burma in decades, the development of a democracy and human rights movement. Do INGOs support the vision for Burma articulated by Aung San Suu Kyi and the NLD? If so, how will INGOs work to support her?

INGO contact with the NLD can be explored creatively in the future through:

- correspondence and discussion via third parties: embassies (some of whom have expressed their willingness to assist); Burmese close to the NLD; outside INGO envoys from peak bodies; INGO envoys from outside Burma who could enter Burma on tourist visas and visit the NLD discreetly
- discreet meetings with NLD Central Committee members or the NLD Social Welfare Committee, perhaps under the protective umbrella of embassy staff's homes
- meet directly with Aung San Suu Kyi
- collaboration by INGOs inside and outside of Burma to organize a short briefing and training on development approaches by INGOs for the NLD. Such training could be organized outside Burma and presented by third party INGO personnel who enter on tourist visas and who are not ostensibly linked to those inside.

INGOS IN BURMA—A HOLISTIC APPROACH

INGOs inside Burma could think more about the overall social movement for change in Burma and how their work relates to it. A fourth generation approach is required. Areas to be explored further include:

- INGO support for embryonic civil society
- INGO exploration of human rights

- an overarching model for social change which focuses on empowerment of communities.

Civil Society

An essential problem facing INGOs in Burma is the lack of civil society. We see this in the limited range of local partners to work with, so many INGOs work with the same GONGOs. The question is how to develop strategies which facilitate the strengthening of thinking which underpins civil society. The political scientist and Burma expert, David Steinberg, observes:

> Since 1962, the military has destroyed civil society in Burma. There has been an obvious systematic, and successful effort to control, co-opt, or eliminate any organisation that had potential for societal influence beyond those at the most local level—village or ward Buddhist temples. Those few private organizations that were allowed to exist in the BSPP era became essentially parastatal in nature. Although under the current regime, the State Law and Order Restoration Council (SLORC), there is a far wider range of ostensibly private organisations and private political parties are titularly allowed to exist, there are none that escape government surveillance and control. . . . In a sense, the SPDC has attempted to recreate civil society in its own manner while suppressing alternative possibilities.[49]

On this basis, INGOs should not formally work with GONGOs. By formally working with these bodies, particularly USDA, INGOs tacitly support and strengthen the control of state structures over the community and at the expense of weaker local INGOs and church and Buddhist *sangha* networks. While the reality is that INGOs may draw in GONGOs personnel for training in the future, this should always be on an individual basis and never at the institutional level. INGOs should focus their energies on assisting the already well-trained personnel in weaker bodies such as the YMCA, Myanmar Council of Churches and others. While INGOs will lose some opportunities in terms of the reach of the GONGO networks, it is a far better outcome that INGOs attention and resources be focused on training communities with basic health skills where they are not organized by parastatal structures.

Human Rights

The struggle to achieve comprehensive development and respect for human rights in Burma requires that both humanitarian relief, and community development and advocacy, be undertaken. Tolerance on both sides of the NGO debate is needed, for all share one commonality—nobody wishes to see the army's rule perpetuated. One of the arguments advanced for INGOs not to work in Burma is the SPDC's record of human rights abuse. All too often however, it is forgotten that human rights are upheld in the UN system as being indivisible, inalienable and universal. If we take the principle of indivisibility seriously—that economic, social, and cultural rights are as important as civil and political rights—then we should concede that bodies that specialize in improving economic and social human rights do have a role in operating inside Burma. They may differ in their style from those bodies that focus on advocacy around civil and political human rights abuses but it is an equally important and needed role. Focusing on one set of people's needs cannot be at the expense of ignoring others; there is a need for all INGOs, development and advocacy, to acknowledge their different but complimentary work.

Development INGOs inside Burma need to examine options for indirectly facilitating improvement of civil and political human rights. This requires development INGOs to more actively educate themselves on the linkages between development and human rights and how this is executed in practice, rather than just making the assertion (as many do) that because their work is concentrated in the economic and social sphere that they are necessarily improving human rights. Many development INGOs could fruitfully explore how human rights might be more substantially articulated in programming. There is a trend in OECD donor governments to promote human rights through development assistance; INGOs need to embrace this trend and make it their own. All too often governments focus on good governance and institutional capacity building when they talk about human rights; INGOs bring experience and intellectual energy for promoting human rights at a grassroots level.

However, some analysts remain skeptical of attempts at grassroots approaches under authoritarian governments. Phillip Alston, the chair of the United Nations Committee on Economic, Social, and Cultural Rights argues:

Participation, in my view, has always been a euphemism for civil and political rights and it has troubled me because it has never been given any precise content by those who use it with reckless abandon in the development debate. Very often it is only applied to the micro level. It is quite unrealistic to pretend that in a country which is fundamentally authoritarian, an agency is going to come in and be able to run a project in a totally participatory manner. This would guarantee a draconian response from the government. Additionally, the communities with which we are often concerned in these contexts are the very ones which have a limited capacity to participate.[50]

Alston argues that the only viable path is support for human rights advocacy:

This leads us back to the need to undertake traditional human rights activities if anything is to be done in order to support those groups which are seeking to promote development at the local and national levels. It gets us back to the need to support and perhaps protect those groups which begin to acquire the power and influence to, not oppose, but rather act as counterweights to the otherwise unchecked power of government.[51]

In this context of having a more explicit human rights focus, there are opportunities for INGOs operating in Burma to explore the following:
- Conduct regional training and workshops for their staff (not just in Burma) on the major human rights instruments and on how the principles contained in the human rights treaties translate in development. For example, the Norwegian branch of Save the Children Fund (SCF) network, Radda Barrnan, has taken a lead role amongst the SCF agencies in promoting the principles in the Convention on the Rights of the Child.
- Contribute funds from other country branches or home locations to support the human rights advocacy of advocacy INGOs outside Burma.
- Gather information on conditions in Burma and do advocacy work through their international branches and partnerships.
- Improve communications between development INGOs and advocacy-based INGOs outside Burma.

- Read and follow advocacy information services, e.g. Burmanet, on PGP encrypted network.
- Develop a reporting system which records needs and violations of social and economic human rights, and raise concerns about needs and violations in areas such as children's rights, where children are often used as forced labor, compelled to be child soldiers (in ethnic armies too), or denied education because of ethnic origin. They could supply this information through their international arms or third-party agencies to UN bodies—UNHCR, ILO, UN Committee on Human Rights, Special Rapporteur for Myanmar, etc.
- Discreetly visit and participate, consult, and share information with forums which are attended by advocacy-based NGO networks such as the Burma Donor's Secretariat and the BBC meetings, or form a new forum combining all of them.

Witnessing

INGOs in Burma are unique in that their presence allows them to adopt a position of "witnessing" the suffering of Burmese and informing the world about it. Many of the activities listed above are encompassed by this concept of witnessing. Witnessing has been practiced by INGOs in Rwanda and the southern Sudan. It is relevant in countries where there is a concealment of information by the government, official sources of information cannot be trusted, and there is a need for speedy and accurate reporting of suffering and abuses. It is a political act and does require an assessment of risk and a high level of cooperation amongst agencies. It works well when the information can be shared and distributed in a protective coalition of INGOs. With the Sudan crisis, INGOs based in Nairobi acted as witnesses through the Association in the Relief of Southern Sudan. The BBC and CCSDPT perform a similar function for Burma in Bangkok. The practical issue might be how agencies in Burma could get information to the BBC and CCSDPT in a confidential manner. For INGOs on the inside to do this, there will have to be more tolerance by outside INGOs of the constraints they work under and a new appreciation that any information provided must absolutely protect the source.

Empowerment

If civil society is to be nurtured in Burma, it is crucial for INGOs to initiate development strategies which foster independent thinking, and democratic structures and management in the communities that they target, including their local staff. Notions of hierarchy need to be broken down and alternative models based on equality explored. An essential role that INGOs can and have played in other countries is breaking through community lethargy engendered by institutional oppression. INGOs can foster confidence in communities to tackle their issues and problems themselves. Undertaking education activities with communities is the key for INGOs to making the transition from humanitarian relief to community development. It is possible (and INGOs are increasingly looking at doing so now) to work more at a village level, with less input from the state (e.g. MSF–Holland has a separate system of health clinics from the government), with loose-knit community networks based around special interests, e.g. well-building, forestry, fishing, and women's health. INGOs are exploring how these groups can be brought together and maintained.

In working with these communities, INGOs need to adopt a broad body of principles on what community development should mean in the Burmese context. While the term "empowerment" cannot be used openly, this must be the outcome of the processes of development. At the grassroots level it is worth bearing in mind the framework of M.D. Anisur Rahman, the developer of Participatory Action Research:

> Empowerment: There is, indeed, no escape from this question . . . A qualitative element of empowerment is control over economic resources; but progress in this matter is by itself no indication of enhanced social power of the underprivileged to assert their developmental aspirations and their freedom to take initiatives for their self development.[52]

More broadly, Rahman argues that development should seek to empower at a societal level and must embody the following principles:[53]

- It must promote *human dignity* and ameliorate abuses of the powerful against others on the basis of economic status, ethnic origin, color, caste, etc.
- Social development must progress towards genuine *popular democracy*—"a system whereby the broad masses of the people

have an effective voice in their shaping of macro policy and the conduct of public affairs."

- Cultural diversity requires that a developing society encourages the authentic development of people's cultures: ". . . to interact with each other for mutual enrichment rather than for domination." Rahman argues that social development ". . . necessarily implies people's development at the grass roots, for otherwise only an abstract concept, e.g. the nation state, may be promoted."

Again, if development INGOs see this model as a desirable long-term outcome of their work, they should use it in evaluating their projects. If there is a clear increase in SPDC restrictions on INGOs promoting these values for the long term, then INGOs should reconsider their presence in Burma.

This holistic approach to human rights and development in Burma will not bring quick or easy results, but it should be implemented because it relates to fundamental questions of how development actually occurs. There needs to be a lot more discussion of the constraints and opportunities for development in Burma, beyond the few issues flagged in this paper. Aung San Suu Kyi has emphasized the crucial importance of dialogue. This is also required amongst all the parties in the continuing NGO debate.

APPENDIX: HEALTH PROFILE OF BURMA

MALNUTRITION: UNICEF estimates nearly half of all primary school–age children in Burma are malnourished, not only young children in rural areas but also those in urban slums.[54] Low energy and low protein intakes are reflected in high levels (30.5% weight for age) of Protein Energy Malnutrition (PEM) among children under three years. The estimated age of stunting, which indicates past or chronic malnutrition, has increased from 29.1% in 1990 to 40.5% in 1991. Vitamin A deficiency is present in 30–44% of primary school–age children. Anemia effects performance coordination and increases susceptibility to infection.[55]

IODINE DEFICIENCY: Goiter is the most visible sign of inadequate iodine intake. A total goiter prevalence of 5% or more constitutes a public health threat. The prevalence of goiter among school children is 38.1% and is exceptionally high in Shan and Kachin states—66% in the latter. A social mobilization campaign to achieve universal salt iodination has been undertaken by UNICEF, the Ministry of Health, the Myanmar Red Cross and several other GONGOs and local NGOs.

VACCINE PREVENTABLE DISEASES: The mortality rate among children aged 5–15 years is 2 per 1000. Most of these deaths are preventable. Vaccine preventable diseases which take a high toll include tuberculosis, tetanus and measles, which are associated with pneumonia and other acute respiratory infections. Neonatal tetanus is a problem, with 125 neonates contracting tetanus in 1993 and 25 dying. Immunization covers 68% of women. Vaccination against measles was introduced in 1985 and has resulted in a decline in cases to 1220 cases in 1993. Some mortality may be under-reported due to confusion with complications with pneumonia. UNICEF is instituting a Vitamin A program alongside measles vaccination. Poliomyelitis or polio virus is endemic but is on the decline; 45 cases were reported in 1993 but these are considered to be an underestimate as there is no laboratory capacity to detect acute cases in Burma.

UNIVERSAL CHILD IMMUNIZATION (UCI) has been initially successful with an 80% coverage rate of 210 of Burma's 320 townships. However, with rural areas more difficult to reach, UCI is probably only 60%. Constraints on UCI include military/security restrictions to border areas, no electricity for maintaining the cold chain, transportation difficulties, and shortage of health staff.

ACUTE RESPIRATORY INFECTIONS are the single greatest cause of infant and child mortality in Burma, accounting for an estimated 24% of all deaths. Neonatal pneumonia accounted for 23.1% of all infant deaths in 1990. Viral respiratory infections are common during the winter months of November to January and the rainy season of mid-May to November. The World Health Organization (WHO), UNICEF, and the Ministry of Health are undertaking a public awareness prevention campaign and training with midwives. There is a lack of antibiotics in health clinics.

DENGUE FEVER: Dengue hemorrhagic fever poses a serious treat to people living in urban slums—many forcibly relocated people. Mortality and morbidity is highest in children under fifteen: 20–30% per 100,000.

DIARRHEA: Diarrheal diseases are the second leading cause of death among children under five, accounting for 18% of mortalities. Mortality increases when it is complicated by malnutrition and other diseases. Oral Rehydration Therapy (ORT) has been available in Burma and is used in a comprehensive Control of Diarrheal Diseases Program (CDD) which has been running for ten years. UNICEF supports the production of oral rehydration salts but knowledge is low outside urban areas.

MALARIA: Malaria is the major cause of illness and death in Burma. Clinically suspected malaria cases treated as out-patients numbered about 600,000 annually, and in-patients numbered about 130,000 annually. Twenty-two percent of all deaths in hospital are caused by malaria. The incidence of malaria is particularly high in Chin and Arakan (Rhakine) states, Irrawaddy division and along the border with Thailand. P. Falciparum is the most common form with around 80% predominance. Two peaks of transmission are observed from April to July and from October to December. Infection is aggravated by complex population movements—refugees and migrant laborers—and treatment is hindered by drug resistance to chloroquine and mefloquine. UNICEF estimates that the real incidence of malaria could be 6–7 times greater than conservative WHO estimates.

CHOLERA: There has been an upsurge in cholera outbreaks in Burma, especially during the rainy season. Notification of cases is poor and mortality is high at 3% of those referred to health centers. A new strain of Vibrio cholera is spreading through Southeast Asia and has reached Burma where there is no existing immunity.

TUBERCULOSIS: TB is a priority health area and is on the increase in Burma, along with HIV/AIDS, affecting the most economically productive age group (15–59 years). The National TB Control Program found that most patients tested in the north were suspected of having HIV. TB is now the second leading cause of mortality at 12.1%.

HIV/AIDS: Due to large increases in drug production in Burma the incidence of intravenous drug use (IVDUs) has increased. New transport routes and the movement of migrant labor have all increased the incidence of HIV and it is spreading out amongst young people, fishermen, truck drivers, traders, day laborers, and miners, as well as the women who are their wives and partners. Sentinel surveys in Kachin State have shown an incidence of 95% amongst IVDUs, 73% in Rangoon, and 84% in Mandalay. In 1995, 570 AIDS cases were reported but this may well be an underestimation of the "blackspot disease."

Due to social and cultural reasons, condom use remains low and the government's policy is subtly pro-natalist. The recently ousted minister for health was cited as a big impediment to effective community awareness programming. The Department of Health and INGO strategy has been to focus on border crossing points and routes—Kawthaung, Kentung/Tachilek, Myawaddy, and most recently around the gem mines in Kachin State. General community awareness programs have been undertaken by the department, INGOs, GONGOs, and local NGOs and churches in urban areas, and with health workers.

WATER SUPPLY AND SANITATION: Unsanitary methods of waste disposal, unhygienic practices, and unsanitary environments amongst much of the Burmese population results in a high incidence of water- and excreta-related diseases such as diarrhea, dysentery, trachoma, etc. Thirty-nine percent of the rural population and 36% of the urban dwellers have access to safe drinking water. Only 35% of the rural population and 39% of urban dwellers have sanitary living conditions. Burma's rainfall is 2000mm annually, but while rain is abundant, coverage is very poor. Some highland areas, the delta, and areas along the major rivers have sufficient water for irrigating two to three crops per year.[56]

The Department of Health and UNICEF have developed a program "Sanitation for all by the year 2000" to achieve universal access to safe drinking water, universal sanitation, and reduction of diarrhea and mortality of children under five by 25% and 50% respectively.

NOTES

1. SLORC was renamed the State Peace and Development Council in November 1997.

2. Action Contre la Faim (ACF); Australian Red Cross (withdrew Feb '97); The Association of Medical Doctors of Asia for Better Quality Life for a Better Future (AMDA); Adventist Development and Relief Agency (ADRA); Association Francois Xavier Bagnoud (AFXB); Bridge Asia (Japan) (BAJ); CARE Myanmar; Groupe de Recherche et d'Echanges Technologiques (GRET); Marie Stopes International; Mèdecins du Monde (MdM); Medecins Sans Frontieres (MSF–Holland); OISCA International; Population Services International (PSI); Save the Children Fund UK; Save the Children USA; PACT; World Concern; World Vision Myanmar.

3. David C. Kortens, *Getting to the 21st Century: Voluntary Action and the Global Agenda* (West Hartford:___ 1990) pp. 114–123.

4. Mike Crooke, "Development Dilemmas: Understanding the difficulties of practical altruism," ACFOA development issues 1, August 1997, p.9.

5. Confidential NGO report #1

6. Ibid.

7. Kortens, op cit., p. 121.

8. Ibid., p.124.

9. The holding of the 1990 elections and the failure of the SLORC to honor its results, further alerted the international system to the nature of Burmese authoritarianism. The election results were given international endorsement in successive UN General Assembly Resolutions and human rights abuse in Burma was scrutinized by the international community through the establishment, in 1991, of the office of the UN Special Rapporteur on Myanmar to inform the secretary general of the United Nations about human rights abuses and political developments. Since 1993 there have been increasingly strong resolutions passed unanimously by the UN General Assembly. The International Labor Organization has commenced a Commission of Inquiry into the SPDC's use of forced labor and the attention and policy of many governments' human rights policies is well-focused on Burma. Other political networks focusing on Burma include the trade unions (e.g. ICFTU), and European, American, and Korean political foundations (e.g. Friedrich Naumann Foundation, Open Society Institute, and the Forum of Leaders in the Asia Pacific).

10. Comparing the democracy movement with civilian protest in Burma prior to 1988 indicates an evolving social movement. Intense but localized student and worker protests against the dictatorship of General Ne Win in 1962, 1963, 1974–76, and 1987 failed to attract mass civilian support and rarely made more than news summaries in the global media. Even the massive 1988 pro-democracy uprising which encompassed far more towns and people than similar student-led protests in China the following year, was received by the world with surprise and little media coverage, so used was the world to the lack of information and isolation of Burma.

11. Reported under the title "Burma—a new test case for the UN," in the *Nation* (Thailand), 30/3/92. See also ICVA [International Council of Voluntary Agencies] Mission to Burma Report, Canberra, 1993, p. 7; and paper presented at Oxford in December 1991, by UNICEF director Rolf Carriere, "Responding to Myanmar's silent emergency: the urgent case for international humanitarian relief and development assistance." In the heat of the debate about whether INGOs should or shouldn't enter, many of Grant's more interesting ideas about a comprehensive approach to development—particularly initiatives to tackle the political situation—were missed. In hindsight, perhaps ideas such as a the creation of a temporary regional and international police and observer force in Burma to supervise a transition of power were far too optimistic. Nevertheless his comprehensive approach to development, tackling political conditions, as well as the social and economic conditions, was sound.

12. Rollason was also the executive director of the Australian Council for Overseas Aid (ACFOA) at the time.

13. ICVA, op. cit., pp. 7–8.

14. Ibid., pp. 22–28.

15. Ibid., pp. 55–59. The mission made twelve recommendations focused mainly on multilateral responses to the political situation and the refugees in Thailand and Bangladesh

16. Ibid., pp.53–4.

17. Maise Warburton, Response to the International Council of Voluntary Agencies (ICVA) Report "Mission to Burma"—The Resumption of Aid to Burma, 1993.

18. In response to the ICVA report, the Australian Council for Overseas Aid and the Burma

NGO Forum held a conference; see ACFOA, *Burma: The Silent Emergency—The Report of a Conference held in Sydney on 28 May 1993*, 1993.

19. Ibid. For their respective speeches, see pp. 4–8, and pp. 9–16.

20. ACFOA, *Silent Emergency*, op cit, pp. 23–26.

21. Ibid., p. 24.

22. Ibid., pp.27–30.

23. Ibid., p. 30.

24. In 1995, ACFOA established a Burma project in its Human Rights Office in Melbourne, which convened several forums on the role for agencies inside Burma; however, its focus is primarily on human rights advocacy. See the following ACFOA Burma project publications:

(a) *Repatriation of Burmese Refugees from Thailand and Bangladesh*, March 1996;

(b) *Daw Aung San Suu Kyi, the SPDC and initiatives for Burma's future*, April 1996;

(c) *Slave Labour in Burma: an Examination of the SPDC's Forced Labour Polices*, May 1996;

(d) *Holidays in Burma* [pros and cons of tourism], November 1996; and

(e) *Human Rights Abuse in Burmese Prisons by Win Naing Oo*, December 1996.

25. Similarly, ACFOA and the Australia Burma Council held a symposium on Burma at Parliament House in October 1995 which was almost entirely focused on the political situation, and the one workshop on HIV/AIDS elicited strong community opposition to INGOs working inside Burma. See ACFOA, *Daw Aung San Suu Kyi. the SPDC and initiatives for Burma's Future: seminar proceedings*, April 1996, pp. 64–5.

26. National Coalition Government of the Union of Burma, Office of the Prime Minister, *Humanitarian and Political Intervention in Burma*, undated.

27. Burma NGO Forum, *Operational Strategies for Australian NGOs in Burma*, Working Draft as of 30 June 1995. Burma Peace Foundation, *Caveats, Cautions and Stringent Conditions (On the Suggestion that NGOs should go into Burma)*, October 1995.

28. Since 1995, Japanese ODA has resumed on a case-by-case basis on debt forgiveness and a US$ 2.3 million funding window for grassroots initiatives by NGOs for 42 projects. The cautious Japanese move towards restoration of ODA contrasts with continuing Western resistance to restoring ODA. There will be extensive lobbying of the UK in its 1998 presidency of the EU on continuing ODA bans and introducing other sanctions.

29. For example, in Australia, World Vision and Australian Red Cross lobbied the government and in September 1993, a funding window was introduced for HIV/AIDS and in March 1994, this funding was expanded to include support for maternal and child health services.

30. WVA funded a HIV/AIDS project coordinator under the broader work of World Vision Myanmar; Tear Australia directed funds to the US NGO, World Concern in Kachin State; ARC worked in partnership with Myanmar Red Cross until March 1997.

31. Article 19, *Fatal Silence? Freedom of Expression and the Right to Health in Burma*, London, July 1996.

32. The UN agencies in Burma are far more important in size and the level of their funding than INGOs. UN agencies, such as United Nation's Children's Fund (UNICEF), United Nations High Commission for Refugees (UNHCR), World Health Organization (WHO), World Food Program (WFP), and United Nations Development Program (UNDP) are taking a lead roles in development, in the areas of water supply and sanitation, primary education, refugee repatriation, HIV/AIDS, and health and nutrition.

33. It helps, according to some, to cultivate the favors of Daw Khin Win Shwe, the vice president of Myanmar Maternal Child Welfare Association and the wife of Khin Nyunt (it is not know if any INGOs have actually done this). Khin Nyunt personally intervened on behalf of one INGO ordered out in 1997, and in doing so overruled the Minister of Health.

34. Confidential, Australian NGO report #2.

35. Some INGOs now believe that the MOU is not the outcome, but rather a letter of understanding which gives permission to operate.

36. Confidential NGO report # 2.

37. Confidential Australian NGO report #1.

38. Confidential interview with former aid worker.

39. It is important to note that Burma-focused relief and development INGOs in Thailand do not criticize the Thai government openly either, lest it jeopardize their ongoing presence and work with refugees, however they do have other discreet means of raising their concerns, not available to their colleagues inside Burma. Moreover the Burma Donor Secretariat should extend invitations to attend its meetings to all INGOs in Burma.

40. CARE and WVM cite in their reports MMCWA and MMA as NGOs and as potential implementing partners. SCF UK has, with OXFAM UK funding, resourced the MMCWA newsletter on the basis that health education material is included.

41. For this reason, Australian Red Cross withdrew from its relationship with MRC in February 1997.

42. MMWCA brochure, "Birth Spacing Projects, Project to Enhance All Reproductive lives (PEARL)."

43. World Vision, *An Introduction to World Vision Myanmar*, Update, June 1996; p. 16.

44. Local NGOs include: National Council of YMCAs, YWCA, Insein Maternal and Child Development Center. Religious Community development/social welfare activities are carried out by: Catholic Bishops Conference of Myanmar, Hindu Central Board, Myanmar Baptist Convention, Myanmar Council of Churches, Myanmar Christian Health Workers Association, Salvation Army, Young Men's Buddhist Association; Zeenat Islam Boy's Home and Educational Society, Muslim Free Hospital and Medical Relief Society.

45. Martin Smith, "Humanitarian and Development Aid to Burma," *Burma Debate,* July/August 1994, pp. 16–21.

46. KIO Central Committee, Standing Commitment, 10/8/94.

47. Author's interview with Catholic Church officials, Rangoon, 1997.

48. Interview by Denise Nicholls, Rangoon, February 1998, available from ACFOA, Canberra, Australia.

49. David Steinberg, "The Union Solidarity and Development Association: Mobilisation and Orthodoxy in Myanmar," in *Burma Debate,* Jan/Feb 1997.

50. Philip Alston, "The rights framework and development assistance," in *Development Bulletin* 34, August 1995, pp. 9–12.

51. Ibid.

52. M.D. Anisur Rahman, *People's Self-Development: Perspectives on Participatory Action Research*, Dhaka 1993, pp. 205–211.

53. Ibid., pp. 210–11.

54. This information appears in UNICEF (1995), op. cit., p.53.

55. A 1991 National Nutrition Center survey identified that stunting at the age for school entry was worse in the following areas (names in brackets are Burmanized): Chin State 49%, Karen State (Kayah) 54.3%, Karenni (Kayin) State 43.9%, Mergui division (Magway) 41.5%, Mon State 46.1%, Sagaing division, 41.6%, southern Shan State 49.1%.

56. Burma is divided into four zones for water supply:

Dry zone: central Burma, less than 1000mm rainfall annually and 46% coverage; shortages during the dry season. Mainly used are tube wells and hand pumps, and small dams and ponds.

Lower Burma: 37% ground water located near the surface and tapped using small ponds and wells.

Delta and coastal areas: rainwater common because of high salinity; 23% water coverage.

Hill region in north and northeast: 5% coverage, gravity systems used to tap perennial springs.

ACRONYMS

ABSDF	All Burma Students' Democratic Front
AFPFL	Anti-Fascist People's Freedom League
ASEAN	Association of Southeast Asian Nations
BADP	Border Area Development Program
BSPP	Burma Socialist Program party
CPB	Communist Party of Burma
DAB	Democratic Alliance of Burma
DKBA	Democratic Karen Buddhist Army
GONGO	Government-Organized Non-Governmental Organization
INGO	International Non-Governmental Organization
KDA	Kachin Defence Army
KIO	Kachin Independence Organization
KNLP	Kayan New Land Party
KNPP	Karenni National Progressive Party
KSNLF	Karenni State Nationalities Liberation Front
KNU	Karen National Union
MMA	Myanmar Medical Association
MMCWA	Myanmar Maternal and Child Welfare Association
MOU	Memorandum of Understanding
MRC	Myanmar Red Cross
MTA	Mong Tai Army
NCGUB	National Coalition Government of the Union of Burma
NCUB	National Council of the Union of Burma

NDA	New Democratic Army
NDF	National Democratic Front
NGO	Non-Governmental Organization
NLD	National League for Democracy
NMSP	New Mon State Party
ODA	Official Development Aid
PLSP	Palaung State Liberation Party
PNO	Pao National Organization
SLORC	State Law and Order Restoration Council
SPDC	State Peace and Development Council
SSA	Shan State Army
SSNLO	Shan State Nationalities Liberation Organization
SSPP	Shan State Progressive Party
SURA	Shan United Revolutionary Army
UNDP	United Nations Development Progam
UNHCR	United Nations High Commission for Refugees
UNLD	United Nationalities League for Democracy
UPNO	Union Pao National Organization
USDA	Union Solidarity and Development Association
UWSP	United Wa State Party
WHO	World Health Organization

BURMA CENTER NETHERLANDS (BCN)

BCN is an information and lobby center. It aims to raise awareness in the Netherlands and the EU about the situation in Burma and strives towards European support for democratization in Burma. In this context BCN has established a close working relationship with national and EU policy makers, politicians, NGOs, and the media. BCN aims to contribute to a meaningful dialogue between the various actors in the Burmese political arena. BCN has been officially registered as a foundation under Dutch law since 1993.

Paulus Potterstraat 20
1071 DA Amsterdam
The Netherlands
phone: 31 20 671 6952
fax: 31 20 671 3513
e-mail: bcn@xs4all.nl
webpage: http://www.xs4all.nl/~bcn

TRANSNATIONAL INSTITUTE (TNI)

TNI is an international network of activist-scholars committed to critical analyses of the global problems of today and tomorrow, with a view to providing intellectual support to those movements concerned to steer the world in a democratic, equitable, and environmentally sustainable direction. TNI has been officially registered as a foundation under Dutch law since 1973.

The Asia Program of TNI studies EU Asia policy and its impact on development and democratization in Asia and gives particular attention to the EU-ASEAN and ASEM forums.

Paulus Potterstraat 20
1071 DA Amsterdam
The Netherlands
phone: 31 20 662 6608
fax: 31 20 675 7176
e-mail: tni@worldcom.nl
e-mail for TNI's Asia Program: tni-asia@worldcom.nl
webpage: http://www.worldcom.nl/tni